Mariner's Compass Quilts

New Quilts from an Old Favorite

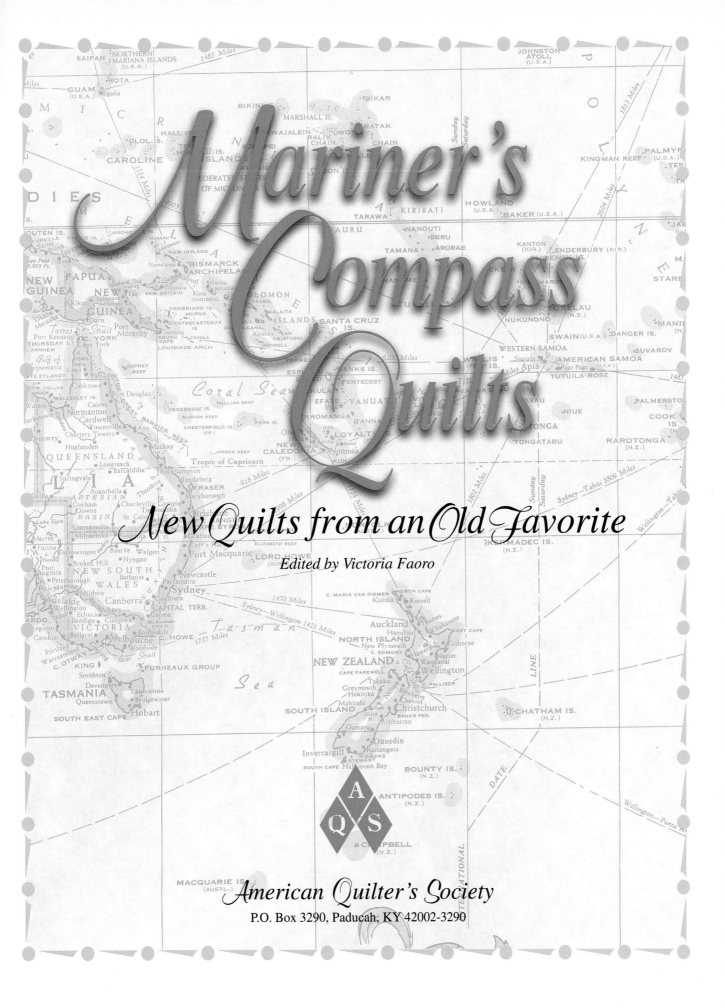

Mariner's Compass Quilts

New Quilts from an Old Favorite

Edited by Victoria Faoro

American Quilter's Society

P.O. Box 3290, Paducah, KY 42002-3290

Located in Paducah, Kentucky, the American Quilter's Society (AQS), is dedicated to promoting the accomplishments of today's quilters. Through its publications and events, AQS strives to honor today's quiltmakers and their work – and inspire future creativity and innovation in quiltmaking.

EXECUTIVE EDITOR: JANE R. MC CAULEY

CONTRIBUTING EDITOR: VICTORIA A. FAORO

BOOK DESIGN AND ILLUSTRATIONS: TERRY WILLIAMS

COVER DESIGN: JENNIFER DAVIS

PHOTOGRAPHY: CHARLES R. LYNCH
UNLESS OTHERWISE NOTED

Library of Congress Cataloging-in-Publication Data

Mariner's Compass Quilts : New Quilts from an Old Favorite
/ edited by Victoria Faoro.
p. cm.
ISBN 0-89145-797-6
1. Quilting – patterns. 2. Patchwork – Patterns. 3. Compass in art.
I. Faoro, Victoria.
TT835.M2723 1997   97-12180
746.46' 041–dc21   CIP

Additional copies of this book may be ordered from: American Quilter's Society,
P.O. Box 3290, Paducah, KY 42002-3290 @ $16.95. Add $2.00 for postage & handling.

Copyright: 1997 Museum of the American Quilter's Society

Dedication

*This book is dedicated to quiltmakers of all
times and all places, whose works continue
to inspire and delight.*

Table of Contents

Preface

This book has been developed in conjunction with an annual Museum of the American Quilter's Society (MAQS) contest and exhibit entitled "New Quilts from Old Favorites." Dedicated to honoring today's quilter, MAQS has created this contest to recognize and share with others the fascinating array of interpretations that can grow out of a single traditional quilt pattern.

A brief introduction to the contest is followed by a presentation of the 18 finalists, including the five winners of awards. Full-color photographs of the quilts are accompanied by their makers' comments, which provide fascinating insights. Full-size templates for the traditional pattern enable anyone to make a Mariner's Compass quilt, minus the work of having to draft the templates needed. The tips, techniques, and patterns contributed by the winning contestants make a wide range of quilts easier to execute in fabric.

It is our hope that this combination of outstanding quilts, full-size patterns, and instructional information will inspire as many outstanding quilts as the original contest did – adding new contributions to this pattern's continuing tradition.

For information about entering the current year's contest write:

MAQS
P.O. Box 1540
Paducah, KY 42002-1540

The Sponsors

A special thanks goes to the corporations whose generous support has made this contest, exhibit, and book possible:

FABRIC TRADITIONS

Fairfield
Quality Polyester Products for Home and Industry

JANOME
NEW HOME®

The Contest

This publication grows out of an annual international contest sponsored by the Museum of the American Quilter's Society. Entitled, "New Quilts from an Old Favorite," this contest encourages quiltmakers to develop innovative quilts using a different traditional pattern each year. The theme for 1997 was the traditional Mariner's Compass pattern.

The only design requirement for quilts entered in the contest was that the quilt be recognizable in some way as related to the Mariner's Compass. The quilt also had to be a minimum of 50" in each dimension and not exceed 100" in any one dimension, and it had to be quilted. A quilt could only be entered by the person who made it, and had to have been completed after December 31, 1991. Many exciting interpretations of this traditional pattern were submitted by quilters from around the world. From these entries were selected the 18 quilts featured in both this publication and the traveling exhibition.

The Mariner's Compass pattern has been the basis of many spectacular quilts. This pattern, believed to be based on the artwork on nautical maps and charts, offers special challenges for accurate drafting of its points, of which there are often as many as 32 in a single compass. But the spectacular results have proved well worth the effort for quilters through the ages.

The design's appearance and names vary depending on how large the inner circle is in relation to the outer circle. The larger the inner circle is, the fatter the rays or points become, prompting names such as Sunflower for some variations. Sunrise, Chips and Whetstones, Sunburst, and Sunflower are among the names designating variations of the traditional Mariner's Compass design.

Mariner's Compass

—ॐ—

The many pieces composing the Mariner's Compass design make it a fine candidate for enlargement in quiltmaking. Rather than repeating the design in many smaller blocks, beautiful quilts have also been created with a central compass, sometimes even as a Medallion-style center. Few blocks hold up well for that type of enlargement.

This design has continued to be used in the twentieth century, with patterns for appliquéd versions published in the 1930's and 1940's and pieced versions continuing to be created. Judy Mathieson's glorious 1980's and 1990's renditions of the pattern and her workshops on its design have inspired many quilters around the country to tackle its beautiful elongated points.

In some cases the quilts entered in this contest were projects that had already been underway at the time the contest was announced; in other cases they had already been completed. A number of quilts entered in the competition were inspired by the contest theme. Some of the quilters commented that they had made Mariner's Compass quilts in the past, but this was their first use of the pattern in an innovative way. This contest provided just the incentive they needed.

Some of the quilters in this contest have retained much from the traditional design, modifying only slightly the pieced structure and usual use of the design. Other quilters have boldly moved in new directions, re-interpreting the design quite dramatically. The quilts are a wonderful reminder of the latitude that traditional patterns offer quiltmakers. These patterns are there to be followed to whatever degree the maker wishes. And regardless of the degree of modification, the results can be very spectacular.

The Winners

Debbie Hern
Dousman, Wisconsin
Cosmosis

Gene P. H. Ives
Alexandria, Virginia
Crossing the Bar

Ans Schipper-Vermeiren
Hagestein, The Netherlands
Compass(ion) Flowers

Nancy Lambert
Mequon, Wisconsin
Star Flower

Suzi Thomas McPherson & Brenda Smallwood Horton
Van Buren, Arkansas
Charting Courses through Time

and Their Quilts

Corinne Appleton

Ruth Cattles Cottrell

Mary Jo Dalrymple & Paulette Peters

Janet Duncan Dignan

Mary L. Hackett

Jo Anna Johnson

Chris Lynn Kirsch

Yoshiko Kobayashi

Susan Mathews

Judith Thompson

Elsie Vredenburg

Sylvia A. Whitesides

Kathy Young

Cosmosis

72" x 72", 1996
Commercial & hand-dyed cottons & silks
Machine pieced, hand appliquéd, machine quilted
& machine embellished

Debbie Hern

— DOUSMAN, WI —

My Quiltmaking

Over ten years ago I began quilting primarily because it was one of the only handcrafts that I hadn't yet tried. I think that one of the reasons I continue to quilt is that it satisfies so many of my creative urges. I like sewing and love both the colors and textures of fabrics. And I can incorporate so many of the other crafts I enjoy in my quilts.

In 1992 I took a workshop taught by Libby Lehman. Up until that point I had known that there were "art" quilts, but I'd never seen one other than in books. Libby's use of fabrics and colors and her innovative techniques really inspired me. Libby's guidance on my first tentative steps into innovative quiltmaking was invaluable. It was a turning point from which I've never looked back.

I usually work with bright primary colors and lots of black and white. I also tend to stick to a block format, and somehow most of my quilts turn out to be square instead of rectangular. This is only the second contest in which I've entered a quilt.

My Mariner's Compass Quilt

I'd wanted for some time to make a quilt using the Mariner's Compass pattern. When I heard about the MAQS contest, I decided to go for it.

For me, making a Mariner's Compass quilt was like the best and the worst of quilting experiences. This was my first experience working with the Mariner's Compass pattern, and I found it very challenging. Had I known how time consuming this project would be, I would probably never have started it. Once I was committed, however, I made myself get through the difficult or tedious parts somehow. When the quilt was finished, I was happy that I hadn't given up. Thank goodness for the anonymous quilter who helped us by inventing paper foundation piecing!

Designing is something that I have always enjoyed. I hope that people recognize my love of color, design, and texture, and enjoy looking at my quilts for these qualities. I would like to make another quilt based on this design, but not right away!

"I love using hand-dyed fabrics in quilts. A very beautiful piece of Melody Johnson's hand-dyed pima cotton was used for the centers of a lot of the Mariner's Compass blocks in my quilt, including the center circle and rays of the large central compass."

See page 88 for full-size patterns and drafting information.

Crossing the Bar

56" x 56", 1996
Cottons, lamé, wool batting
Hand pieced & hand quilted

Gene P. H. Ives

— ALEXANDRIA, VA —

My Quiltmaking

My quilting activity began in around 1991. I had to first retire as a commercial artist, see my children raised and out of the house on their own, and teach my husband how to cook and do the wash. I have been influenced by many in my quilt-making. Every-one I meet becomes an influ-ence, and it's been my experience that quilters are the great-est. I have found Anne Oliver to be one of the most generous with her help.

People will probably not be surprised by this quilt. It's fun to try to "push the envelope," and people are generous to put up with me and my different quilts.

Making quilts is a lark for me. I never really graduated from kindergarten, I love to cut, color, and paste. The possibilities are endless. You know what people say: "God put me on earth to accomplish a certain number of things. Right now I am so far behind, I will never die."

What's my next quilt going to be? It isn't quite ready to hatch, but it's getting there.

My Mariner's Compass Quilt

The MAQS contest inspired my quilt – and my wondering if it would be possible to make a double exposure by using a Mariner's Compass superim-posed on Winslow Homer's painting Eight Bells. (Do you smell the fish sticks?)

To accomplish the design, the pat-tern was drawn full-size on blank newsprint. Each piece in the drawing was numbered and traced on freezer paper, and the pieces were cut apart and used as patterns. Fabrics were cut from the patterns, hand pieced, and hand quilted.

It is my hope that through this quilt people will enjoy the romance of the sea, our early heritage, and the bringing togeth-er of Winslow Homer and Alfred Lord Tennyson, whose verse inspired the title.

This was my first experience with the Mariner's Compass design. I'd like to make one like Judy Mathieson's "Nautical Stars," working with the overlap-ping and gradations of colors – what a challenge that would be!

"Making a mariner's compass was an enjoyable challenge – it was great fun seeing if what had popped into my head was do-able."

See page 66 for tips on templates.

Compass(ion) Flowers

55" x 55", 1996
Silks, cotton batting
Machine pieced & hand quilted

Ans Schipper-Vermeiren

─── HAGESTEIN, THE NETHERLANDS ───

My Quiltmaking

In Holland it rains a lot. One day I took refuge in a shop where the owner had just begun to do patchwork instead of knitting. There I heard of a beginner's patchwork course starting the next day in Amersfoort, which is 40 kilometers or about 25 miles from my own village. I immediately called the shop and luckily I was the last person to be able to join the class. And so I started a beginner's course that September.

Quiltmaking has changed me as a person, making me more self-assured. As I have come to learn what I like in quilts I have become more able to express myself in other parts of my life.

I don't have any plans for working with the Mariner's Compass design again. I do, though, have plans for continuing to work with my silk fabrics.

My dream is to make a very large quilt from small right triangles cut from all my leftover silk. This quilt will be a beautiful garden of flowers.

My Mariner's Compass Quilt

Since so many quilters in Holland have made the Mariner's Compass pattern, I was never inspired to make a quilt using this design until I read about the MAQS contest. Almost immediately I came up with the idea for this quilt.

About six years ago I had made a Mariner's Compass block for a sampler quilt during lessons for my first quilt. Making this Mariner's Compass contest quilt was a daily adventure as I experienced its growth. The experience reminded me of the wonder of flowers developing in the spring.

My friends were surprised by this quilt because the Mariner's Compass design has never really interested me – it is such a formal pattern. I hope people will see the flowers rather than a Mariner's Compass design. The flowers in the corners remind me of a tropical flower which is foreign to Holland but is often used in arrangements – Strelitzia-Reginae (bird of paradise).

"Why do I make quilts? Because I can't stop. I often enter contests because of the challenge, the theme, and a deadline."

Star Flower

51" x 51", 1996

Cottons

Machine pieced & machine quilted

Nancy Lambert

MEQUON, WI

My Quiltmaking

I began quilting about ten years ago. I saw a quilt I wanted to buy but couldn't afford and decided that perhaps I could make my own quilt. I took a class at a local quilt shop and have been buying fabric ever since. I quilt with a group of friends every other week. Working with them has encouraged me to both start and finish more quilts. The past several years I've also entered a few contests, mainly as an additional incentive to finish quilts.

I like the use of fabric and pattern, both of which I have plenty on hand. I really enjoy the way the tones in large-scale prints add dimension and interest to any design. My friends are used to seeing bright and unusual fabrics in my quilts, but this is perhaps my brightest and boldest use of colors yet.

I thoroughly enjoy my quiltmaking, but I would like to have time enough to do more parts of the projects by hand, such as dyeing fabrics, or hand stippling for more texture.

My Mariner's Compass Quilt

This quilt was inspired by a group of large-scale floral prints and the intricacy of the pattern. I wanted to see how a traditional "very precise" pattern would look with "loose" large-scale fabrics. I have enjoyed the way Libby Lehman uses these prints and I may have been influenced by her designs.

This is the first Mariner's Compass pattern I've completed. Usually I use simple Nine-Patch or other "non-pointed" designs. I was planning a quilt for my daughter and wanted to make something in a star pattern. Hearing about the MAQS contest and thinking about a star pattern, I decided to try a Mariner's Compass design. Stitching the design in fabric was a test. This was a difficult pattern to accurately piece, but the result was well worth the challenge.

I find I'm envisioning other Mariner's Compass projects. I would like to make a very traditional piece, along with one where each star resembles a flower.

"I wanted to give a somewhat lighthearted look to a very traditional pattern. I hope viewers enjoy the many combinations of color that keep the eye moving."

See page 68 for tips on using large-scale prints.

Charting Courses through Time

56" x 69", 1996

Cottons, beads, cotton batting

Machine pieced, hand appliquéd & machine quilted

Suzi Thomas McPherson
and
Brenda Smallwood Horton
── VAN BUREN, AR ──

Our Quiltmaking

I began quilting from my mother's love of quilts and the influence of a friendship quilt she made for my marriage. I played with patchwork for over a year before I located my first quilting class eighteen years ago. Most of my early work involved adding patchwork to my daughters' clothing.

Brenda began by sewing doll clothes at age five and has sewn ever since, completing a BS in clothing and textiles. She began quilting in 1975. It was she who introduced me to Belle Point Quilters' Guild, which turned my quiltmaking into a true passion. Brenda and I both relish the history of quilting and feel connected to history and the future through continuing the art form.

Together Brenda and I develop sketches for future quilts. We frequently combine appliqué with a patchwork block with significance in its title, as we both like our work to tell a story. We also love to create landscape quilts.

We continue to study with other quiltmakers and hope to teach more classes ourselves and publish patterns we have created.

Our Mariner's Compass Quilt

The contest was the impetus for the quilt. I had never before considered creating a Mariner's Compass quilt, but I immediately knew that I wanted to make an oval compass star. I started with general sketches of the star radiating out from a lighthouse with rocks and water, but I quickly moved the lighthouse away from the star. The next step was to look for fabric.

I showed a piece of sea-fossil fabric to my partner, Brenda. She loved it, so we started playing around with the idea of the star as a guide for explorations through time. That led to the plan of having the fossils as the base and sea floor, leading up to sea travel noted by the lighthouse, on to space explorations through space-SHIPS. The stars have shown over the earth since creation and have been used as a guide for discovery, and we are always dependent on our past to determine our present and future. The Mariner's Compass in our quilt encourages one to venture on one's own voyage.

"Just as a star reaches in all directions and the compass has led many to new explorations, making this first Mariner's Compass quilt was like charting new design courses in scope, size, and color."

See page 70 for tips on developing a complicated design.

IntergalactiCat

52" x 52", 1996
Cottons, sequins, beads, sequin appliqués
Machine pieced and blanket and buttonhole stitch appliquéd, template pieced, paper pieced,
hand beaded, and sequin appliqué

Corinne Appleton

JACKSONVILLE, FL

My Quiltmaking

*A*fter a false start in 1989, I began quilting in late 1991. Two years of machine difficulties meant that my output was only two quilts produced under high anxiety. Resolving my technical difficulties in 1993 freed me to pursue the many quilts in my head.

From the very first quilt I made, I have had a tendency to "color outside the lines." Completing original work gives me pleasure in a way that is incomparable to my other efforts.

In one way or another, I think every quilt I have ever seen, and hence the maker, has influenced my work. Seeing the technical perfection of Jane Sassaman's quilts has given me the patience to hand-tie and weave hundreds of thread ends on a recent project. Seeing the embellishments and surface design of Jane Burch Cochran has helped me give myself permission to depart from the sometimes rigid "rules" of quiltmaking. As a new quiltmaker I find invaluable the enthusiasm of others whose work I admire.

My Mariner's Compass Quilt

*M*y quilt began with a wonderful polka-dot fabric. I envisioned Mariner's Compass blocks with the polka-dot fabric fooling the eye as it stretched the length of each star point. The original quilt plan involved a four block layout, but after assembling my first block, I realized I had nowhere near enough of my beloved polka dots. I was completely stumped. Attempting to cope with what was now a single block center, I hit every fabric store around. Suddenly I realized the solution was at hand – or rather, at paw. My kitties would go traveling a la Star Trek: The Feline Generation. The star of the show would be my own beloved Max(imum).

I had enough fabric to complete a second block like the first, and I could stretch that block by cutting it in four. This created the illusion of a central star exploding towards the viewer. Of course, the biggest star of all — Max(imum) — says a shy "Hi" from dead center.

"Making a Mariner's Compass quilt was like so many of life's little lessons. I had to re-learn the maxim that says 'test the water before you dive in headfirst.'"

See page 64 for a variation.

Between the Devil and the Deep Blue Sea

76" x 76", 1996

Cottons, some batiks, wool batting

Hand appliquéd, machine pieced & hand quilted

Ruth Cattles Cottrell

IRVING, TX

My Quiltmaking

I began quilting in 1990 after a lifelong progression through all the needlearts. The person who has most influenced my work is my mother, Nadine Childress Cattles, an expert seamstress who taught me to sew and make my clothes when I was ten. Although she had not quilted actively since the 1940s, when she retired in 1990, she began talking about completing a 1930's Dutch Doll quilt that had been given to her mother.

In a needlecrafts store I noticed a photo of a Baltimore Album quilt and decided to make one. I bought Jeana Kimbell's book Reflections of Baltimore, and promptly made all 12 blocks. I even designed a border and started it, too.

What really attracts me to quilting is that this is not some embroidered tea towel. A quilt will be here in 100 years – really a work of art. In my past needlecraft lives, I was notorious for unfinished projects. Not so with quilting.

My Mariner's Compass Quilt

*T*he pattern for this quilt was drafted from a picture in Folk Art *magazine (Winter, 1994/95) of an 1850 – 1870 quilt made by Emiline Barker. I drafted the 30" compass down to 22".

Most Mariner's Compass designs are pieced or appliquéd into a background square, but in this quilt, the cross seams lay directly under the center of each compass star. I appliquéd my own compasses the same way.

The blue leaves in the appliqué blocks and the corner pieces are made from a blue batik fish print. This fabric reminded me of the saying "Caught between the devil and the deep blue sea." I researched the saying and discovered it was a sailor's homily. Early sailing ships had a piece of molding around the hull call the "devil," which caused the waves to break at that point, instead of over the deck. When the sailors had to hang out over the edge of the ship and clean it, they were "caught between the devil and the deep blue sea."

"I think the period 1830 – 1870 was the golden age of quilting. I would like the viewers to remember what it must have been like to create pieces such as this without all the modern gadgets, materials, and fabrics we now have."

See page 62 for tips on constructing a "seamless" top.

Earth Angels

50" x 90", 1995

Commercial and hand-dyed cotton fabrics, embroidery thread, beads, Velcro®, polyester batting
Machine pieced, hand appliquéd, hand quilted, machine quilted, embroidered

Mary Jo Dalrymple
and
Paulette Peters

——— OMAHA and ELHORN, NE ———

Our Quiltmaking

Both Paulette and I began quilting in the 1970's, before quilt shops existed. My quilts have been seen in many exhibits and publications, and Paulette has taught quiltmaking for many years and has had two books published. Both of us have studied with different quilters over the years, and our friendship has been a great joy and inspiration. For this project, we collaborated, with parameters set forth (and sometimes ignored).

The rationale for working jointly on this project was, in Paulette's words, "to experience someone else's creative process, to use the strengths of each, and to spend time together. We determined we would work together – being careful to neither tiptoe nor takeover; we would express ourselves without stifling each other's creativity. We would find a form to work together on one product with equally invested time. In the end we would each own part of the piece."

We accomplished most of our goals; we had fun doing it and we're even better friends!

Our Mariner's Compass Quilt

"Earth Angels" is really seven separate quilts in one. Each of the angel quilts may be hung separately or attached by Velcro® to the display quilt as shown. We have portrayed six realms of nature in our angels: Lunar, Winter, Leafage, Storms, Animal Kingdom, and Star. There are endless possibilities for adding new angels to the collection. Earth angels can be thought of as nature spirits who bring healing energy to the planet, and harmony to the natural order. It is good to think that each animal, each tree, each blade of grass has a guardian angel bending over it, investing it with spirituality. This quilt grew out of experiments with the Mariner's Compass block. I was playing around and the pieces suggested an angel. Knowing Paulette likes angels I constructed a preliminary block and mailed it to her. Paulette found it a "perfect connection between the ethereal idea of angels and the global concept of the compass."

We had talked about a collaboration and this subject resonated with both of us.

"In some angel lores, the guardian of the earth is represented in a circular or wheel form. The circle of a Mariner's Compass was the starting point for our Earth angels, who bring healing energy to the planet, and harmony to the natural order."

See page 102 for full-size patterns and instructions.

Homeward Bound

65" x 76", 1996
Cottons, needle-punched cotton batting
Machine pieced, machine appliquéd & machine quilted

Janet Duncan Dignan

— WEYMOUTH, MA —

My Quiltmaking

I began quilting 13 years ago when our first grandchild was expected. My dear mother taught me to sew and it has been a natural evolution – doll clothes, dresses, curtain, slip-covers, and finally quilts. I have been teaching for nine years, and find every quilter influences my work, class-mates as well as teachers.

At the Vermont Quilt Festival, I have taken classes from the Larry Birds of the quilting world and they have all affected me. I was strongly influenced by a Caryl Bryer Fallert class at MAQS and used some of her techniques to complete my entry in this contest. Quilters should be encouraged to take four- or five-day classes – it's an incredible learning experience.

One of my greatest joys has been teaching four daughters-in-law to quilt. When I started, they put their orders in. I assured them they would get quilts much faster if they made their own. We began classes at my home and had a wonderful show the end of the first year. They are my enthu-siastic home team supporters.

My Mariner's Compass Quilt

A Mariner's Compass is a device for determining direction – with it you can travel around the world and always find your way home. Standing on my deck in early April, the night sky glows with stars that are positioned as they are on my quilt "Homeward Bound" – Orion's Belt is just below my horizon. I had always avoided Mariner's Compass quilt patterns because of all those awful points! My decision to take the plunge and enter the MAQS competition was a catalyst, giv-ing me the freedom to exprress my abilities and test myself beyond normal expectations.

Making a Mariner's Compass was a self-teaching process. If I were working with this design again, I probably would not change it other than to vary the number of points, or scatter the points around, overlapping them or varying their placement in other ways. It being a functional item, I would struggle to "warp" it. I am very anxious to see the contemporary designs created by computer-oriented quilters.

"This was my first entry in a quilt contest. Having been judged a finalist, I'm on cloud nine – a very happy quilter!"

See page 99 for instructions for making "Homeward Bound."

Ancient Mariner: The Purple Empire

58" x 75", 1996
Cottons, lame, upholstery fabric
Machine appliquéd, machine pieced, machine thread
painted and embroidered & machine quilted

Mary L. Hackett

CARTERVILLE, IL

My Quiltmaking

I began quilting in 1987 in order to produce a small wall-hanging for my bathroom. My next piece won a purchase award, and I was off and running.

My quiltmaking has been influenced the most by Penny McMorris. Her suggestion that I look inward for inspiration and strength, perse-vere, and concentrate on producing significant work, has been a continual source of encouragement.

People who know my work would recognize this piece as mine. I have made other pieces employing almost life-size fig-ures, and the border treatment reflects my delight in sponta-neous machine piecing and thread painting. I enjoyed researching "Ancient Mariner: The Purple Empire" and would like to do more "quilts with a bibliography," as one friend has called such quilts. I hope my heart gives out before my eyes and hands do.

I enter contests occasionally, but am trying to participate in fewer of them and concentrate on commissions.

My Mariner's Compass Quilt

The MAQS contest inspired this quilt. The phrase "ancient mariner" from "The Rime of the Ancient Mariner" intrigued me, but I thought of an entirely dif-ferent "ancient mariner" – the Phoenicians, who brought navigational and manufactur-ing skills and spread their culture across the Mediterranean.

I do not generally favor block-style quilts, so I never consid-ered repeating the Mariner's Compass again and again, but sought a way to feature one com-pass in a meaningful way.

My Phoenician merchant actu-ally resembles a modern-day Lebanese man. He wears purple garments of this period, colored with a compound that required an incredible 10,000 snails to produce one gram of dye.

Various relics and hieroglyphs are included in the borders. The compass, which makes it all pos-sible, glows in the hands of my "ancient mariner," a mysterious disk with a star at its heart, fasci-nating him and guiding him on his journeys.

"I regarded the Mariner's Compass literally as a means by which the Phoenicians navigated the Mediterranean, selling their mass-produced glass and rare purple-dyed textiles, spreading their influence through the entire area."

See page 74 for tips on looking for inspiration.

Which Way?

68" x 68", 1996
Hand-dyed cottons, cotton batting
Machine pieced, hand appliquéd & machine quilted
photocopied and screen printed images

Jo Anna Johnson

CARBONDALE, IL

My Quiltmaking

I began quilting over ten years ago as a connection with my past, and I've continued because I enjoy expressing original ideas through this comforting medium. I love both the togetherness and the aloneness of quiltmaking. When I'm at my sewing machine it's my own special world, but the togetherness with other quilters cannot be matched. An area art quilt group is especially supportive and encouraging.

My husband and family are also very understanding. When they see the fabric flying – they know I'm on a roll and let me pursue my project.

People who know me only through my work may be surprised by this quilt's political theme. In the past I've been interested in color and depth illusions, techniques more than content. But my undergraduate degree is in political science and our society's issues have always been important to me.

My Mariner's Compass Quilt

"Which Way?" was inspired by a political discussion several friends were having. One said, "I wish we had a moral compass." That got me thinking about what my moral compass would look like.

The outside border was influenced by a slide presentation on gourds. I had fun brainstorming with friends about possible names and phrases to quilt into the border.

The quilt presents a brief visual history of African-American/white relations through photo images from various manuscript collections at Southern Illinois University at Carbondale's Morris Library Archives and names and phrases related to these images. The quilt shows the different paths we have taken and asks which way should we go now. I hope the quilt expresses a hope for a future in which African-Americans and whites will work together as brothers and sisters of humanity. It's important to remember this is from a white woman's perspective.

"It's unlike me to use such large pieces in a quilt, but they were necessary in this quilt. If I were working with the Mariner's Compass pattern again, I would probably make a smaller compass or fracture the large pieces into smaller ones."

See page 77 for tips on photocopy transfers.

The Way Home

62" x 62", 1996

Cottons, cotton/polyester batting, cotton & metallic thread

Machine pieced, hand appliquéd & machine quilted

Chris Lynn Kirsch

OCONOMOWOC, WI

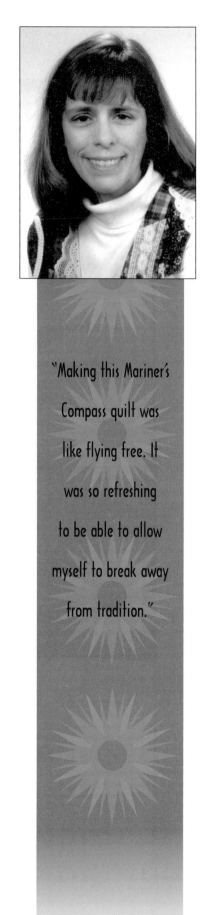

My Quiltmaking

In 1987 my husband was transferred to Madison, WI, where my brother's family lives. My sister-in-law invited me to join her in a quilting class. I had no desire to quilt, but decided to take the class anyway. I will forever be indebted to her.

When our family moved back to the Milwaukee area two years ago I decided to leave my work as a dental hygienist and pursue my passion. I feel so fortunate to be able to spend my time doing what I truly love.

In 1991 I read about an international theme competition and a design idea flashed into my head. It was quite different from the traditional piecing I had been doing, so I told myself to forget about it. A few weeks later I took a workshop with Caryl Bryer Fallert who encouraged me to try to make the quilt. I learned a lot, and was thrilled to have it juried into the show.

I enjoy entering contests and having quilts displayed. Judges' critiques and viewers' comments have improved my quilts and inspired me to continue.

My Mariner's Compass Quilt

A few years ago I devised a method for drafting and foundation piecing a traditional Mariner's Compass design. It simplified the construction so much that I have been asked to teach it as a workshop many times. With each class I made a new round compass, wondering how other shapes would work. This contest gave me permission to design and experiment. I heard about the MAQS competition at the 1996 AQS show and spent part of the ride back to Wisconsin drawing my design. The name, "The Way Home" seemed a fitting title, especially for a Mariner's Compass. I began my fabric search in June and found the border's map fabric at my first stop. The other fabrics just fell into place. I had planned to title this quilt "Any Which Way But Round." However, as the design evolved, it seemed destined to return to round. At times it seemed this quilt was more in control than I was, and that added to the fun.

"Making this Mariner's Compass quilt was like flying free. It was so refreshing to be able to allow myself to break away from tradition."

WWW Navigator's Compass

65" x 65", 1996

Cottons (hand-dyed and commercial), polyester batting, gradation dyed sashiko thread

Hand pieced & hand quilted

Yoshiko Kobayashi
─── KATANO-CITY, OSAKA, JAPAN ───

My Quiltmaking

*I*n my student days and while I was working for a company, I was a member of a picture drawing circle. During that time I also learned dressmaking and kimono sewing. In addition I enjoyed knitting, making fabric bags, and doing hand embroidery on my own. My mother is a dressmaker.

About nine or ten years ago I became involved in quiltmaking. I was inspired by a quilt exhibition in Nagoya. After studying quiltmaking for four years, I moved with my family to Osaka. Since then I have been entirely self-educated as a quilter. During my Nagoya days, I learned how to draw patterns and enjoy making my own quilts. Now, I find I love making designs with fabrics and threads instead of using oil paints.

Now that I'm a self-educated quilter, nobody gives a theme to me. So, I receive quiltmaking motivation from contest themes such as this MAQS contest. I'd like to be challenged more and more.

My Mariner's Compass Quilt

*T*his quilt was made especially for the MAQS contest. I didn't know how to enter until the latter part of July. This left me with only a severely short period of time to complete the quilt because I hand piece and hand quilt.

I love the Mariner's Compass design. I had enjoyed looking at Judy Mathieson's Mariner's Compass book, and longed to make a dynamic quilt like hers.

I had worked with the Mariner's Compass pattern only in a sampler quilt at the beginning of my quilt education. Making a Mariner's Compass quilt was like making my mind think freely as if it were flying in the sky or sailing on the sea during my piecing and quilting.

While I was making this quilt, my husband was absent from his office because of a stress illness. He worked on the World Wide Web with his computer in our home. I thought it was important for us to each have our own compass in mind to guide each of us with our own subject.

"I like traditional patterns and am always thinking about ways I can develop my own expression by using them."

See page 60 for tips on planning quilting designs.

Balance

77" x 77", 1992
Cottons, Thai silks, taffeta
Machine pieced, hand appliquéd & hand quilted

Susan Mathews

—YARRAWONGA, VICTORIA, AUSTRALIA—

My Quiltmaking

I began quilting in 1975, having been an avid weaver and spinner from age 14. By this stage I had completed a teaching course in secondary school art and craft. I worked as a lone quilter for the next six years, entering regional crafts council exhibitions and doing commissions simultaneously with having three children and managing a family retail fabric business. In 1983 I began teaching.

I make quilts purely because I really enjoy playing with pattern and color and seeing a quilt "emerge," change and improve with every little step. I often enter exhibitions in Australia because I enjoy being part of them and like to contribute to organizations to which I belong. I also find that exhibitions provide me with that little push to get something finished. I dream of making a quilt in a really leisurely way with no other demands or deadlines to get in the way. I'd just like to head for the hills for a while and work in an entirely peaceful atmosphere with little else to do but make something beautiful. Talk about a pipe dream!

My Mariner's Compass Quilt

"Balance" was made for the first Melbourne Quilt Exhibition, the theme being "Victoria – Garden State." I wanted to place my appliqué on a subtle pieced background rather than something plain, and I thought that the Mariner's Compass would work well. I had Thai silk scraps and thought that their different textures would be a good way of keeping the background reasonably subtle.

The basic Mariner's Compass behind the appliqué was inspired by "Mariner's Star," a quilt in Shining Star Quilts by Judy Martin. The border design was from Jinny Beyer's The Quilter's Album of Borders and Blocks. The appliqué and quilting designs are original.

The title "Balance" refers to the concept of balance in nature. I wanted to show that the balance of nature is dependent on a myriad of less noticeable elements such as those I have included in the quilting: spiders, butterflies, and caterpillars.

"I love traditional quilts and most of my quilts could probably be classified as traditional, but I try to infuse my own personality through color use and arrangement of design elements."

When This You See, Remember Me
77" x 77", 1996
Vintage cottons, silk
Hand appliquéd, hand pieced & hand quilted with trapunto

Judith Thompson
and Anonymous 19th-century Quilters

WENONAH, NJ

My Quiltmaking

My quilting had two false starts. One start was in 1976 and the second try was in 1979, both with poor results. The sewing machine and I just never got along. Then in 1983 I taught myself the basics of hand piecing and I haven't stopped since. A dedicated hand piecer and hand quilter, it takes me longer to complete a project, but I find the results and the process much more satisfying than I did when using the sewing machine.

I make quilts because I have to! I occasionally enter contests because I like to receive critiques from the judges. I am disappointed when judges' comments are minimal because I learn a lot from them.

I dream of starting the next quilt idea in my head. I often have four to five projects at various stages of completion, so I find I must wait. Sometimes the temptation is just too much and I find myself starting idea number six or seven anyway.

I have used elements of the Mariner's Compass in other projects, but this is my first complete project using it alone.

My Mariner's Compass Quilt

This quilt was inspired by twelve 1840's Vermont signature blocks I had purchased. To complete the quilt, I constructed four new blocks and added an appliqué border, in vintage fabrics. The 1840's blocks show very fine hand workmanship. When I first examined them there appeared to be areas that had been machine stitched. Closer examination revealed they were actually tiny backstitches.

As I quilted, I speculated on the relationships between the individuals represented and their reason for beginning a quilt. Was this to be a presentation quilt for a wedding or a farewell? Was it a fund-raising project that hit on hard times? This 1990's New Jersey quilter will never know the mysteries of the twelve 1840 blocks; but she will, in fact, "Remember Thee."

This quilt brings together the 1840's and the 1990's, and Vermont and New Jersey. An Oak Leaf border (the New Jersey state tree) surrounds the Vermont blocks. The fleur-de-lis at the top is traditional at North on the compass rose.

"I love old quilts, old fabrics, and traditional techniques, so no one was surprised when I incorporated antique blocks in my Mariner's Compass quilt!"

See page 84 for full-size patterns.

Split Rock Sunset

53" x 59", 1996
Cottons, lamé, crepe, tulle, cotton batting
Machine pieced, machine appliquéd & machine quilted

Elsie Vredenburg

TUSTIN, MI

My Quiltmaking

At the insistence of my dad's mother, I began quilting at the age of 17. No one person has particularly influenced my work, but I have picked up bits and pieces from many others. I have received much encouragement from my local guild, the North Star Quilters in Cadillac, Michigan, and from my on-line guild, the Genie On-line Quilters.

Right now I'm involved in a round robin project which includes five American and five New Zealand quilters. I think we're finding that though we live on opposite sides of the world, our lives are very similar.

I make quilts because I like fabric, I enjoy working with my hands, and I like the visual appeal of quilts. I also enter quite a few contests. If nobody entered, we wouldn't have all of those wonderful quilt shows. And, of course, it's great fun to win! I guess I'm a competitor at heart. As with most quilters, there are more projects in my head than I'll ever live long enough to make.

My Mariner's Compass Quilt

The main inspiration for this quilt was the contest itself. Also, I've been working on a series of small lighthouse quilts for which I sell patterns, so my mind has been in a lighthouse mode. I tried incorporating the two thoughts.

I have never been to Split Rock, but people who have been there and have seen the quilt immediately recognized it. I wanted to capture some of the awesome feeling I have when I see pictures of it.

The center portion of the quilt is entirely my own idea, but the border was inspired by an antique strippy quilt brought to our guild meeting for show and tell.

The border also includes a favorite "trick" of mine. To carry the picture out beyond the inner border, I repeat the fabrics in that section of the quilt. For instance, in this one, I used the sky fabrics in the top portion of the border, and the rock and water fabrics in the bottom portion.

"I had never made a Mariner's Compass quilt. I'm not fond of sewing circles, especially appliquéing small centers – you may have noticed that I "cheated," converting the circles to straight lines."

See page 80 for tips on piecing architectural designs.

Sunflowers after Vincent

51" x 65", 1996
Hand-dyed cottons, commercial printed cottons, cotton batting
Machine pieced, hand appliquéd & machine quilted

Sylvia A. Whitesides

LAFAYETTE, IN

My Quiltmaking

I am an at-home mom with three daughters, ages 7, 10, and 13. For me to function as a patient, loving mom, I need my own creative outlet. Since my first daughter was a baby, I have made time for quilting and sewing. My sewing room is also the playroom. This sunflower quilt almost didn't get done in time because my youngest daughter came down with chicken pox just as I was finishing it.

I often enter contests because a contest is like having an assignment. For me that is the best motivation. I also belong to the Professional Art Quilters Alliance of Chicago which meets once a month and has kept me focused and inspired. The group has lots of talented and supportive artists.

When a quilt friend visited while I was working on this quilt she was shocked. "Look at all the yellow fabric piled everywhere." She had never seen such a phenomenon in my sewing room. But I love flowers and gardens, so the design is more familiar to me, though I'd always hand appliquéd flowers before.

My Mariner's Compass Quilt

My Mariner's Compass/ Sunflowers were pieced by machine. Most were machine sewn into the background. The leaves and stems were hand appliquéd onto the background, and the entire quilt was machine quilted. The background quilting design is my own, accomplished with free-motion quilting. I wanted it to look like crackled paint. I had been contemplating doing a Mariner's Compass for the contest but was not interested in the traditional look. A friend suggested a sunflower we saw in a quilt was like a Mariner's Compass. I love Vincent Van Gogh's, Still Life with Sunflowers and had been thinking about trying the sunflowers in appliqué. I decided to instead try piecing Mariner's Compass blocks to look like sunflowers. I experimented with different sizes, different shaped points, different number of points, and different arrangements of color. That's what was most fun about piecing this quilt, challenging myself to come up with different ways to piece each one. Maybe I will try other flowers next time!

> "Making a Mariner's Compass quilt was a real love-hate relationship – like dealing with a 13-year-old daughter can sometimes be. Piecing the compass designs was very difficult."

See page 95 for full-size patterns.

Neil's Compass
71" x 83", 1996
Cottons, cotton batting
Machine pieced & machine quilted

Kathy Young

KALAMAZOO, MI

My Quiltmaking

I became interested in quilt-making because I was drawn to the comfort that a quilt provides and the opportunities for use of color and design in fabric. I was in my twenties and that was nearly twenty years ago. Books, my quilt group, and our guest lecturers have influenced my quiltmaking most. Barbara Caron, Pat Andriatta, Pepper Cory, Marianne Fons, and Helen Kelley have been among those brought in by my group, Log Cabin Quilters. I have limited personal resources, so I am very fortunate to have had these people within my reach.

I love a creative challenge. My first quilt was made using a compass block of Delores Hinson's, one with four curves and twelve points meeting. My first appliqués were of dragons and mythical creatures. Next came Baltimore album blocks.

I am living my dream. I take care of babies eight to nine hours a day, take care of my family's needs, and quilt the remaining time.

My Mariner's Compass Quilt

*M*y son was the inspiration for this quilt. Neil is a talented treasure in my life who sometimes can use guidance. This quilt was not made from a plan. I pretty much "shoot from the hip" when I quilt – I rarely plan. The purpose of the quilt was to enable my son to physically wrap himself in my love. The design has meaning to me and yet it is appealing to a 17-year-old young man. Some of the patterns are from Judy Mathieson's first compass book, but I developed the design myself.

Accuracy in piecing was the greatest challenge in making this Mariner's Compass quilt. Every successful point was an accomplishment. If I were using the design again, I don't think I would change it in any way. It effectively expresses my feelings, so I would use it again if it were appropriate.

Teaching children to quilt is one of my favorite quilting experiences. Every once in a while a child will fall in love with quiltmaking and allow me to share in his/her enthusiasm.

"This was the first contest I have ever entered. I don't usually enter because I give most of my quilts away."

Mariner's Compass Patterns

*I*ncluded in this section are full-size templates for a traditional Mariner's Compass design with 16 points in eight different sizes, ranging from a 5" compass to a 11" compass. Each compass is part of a block 1" larger than its diameter. Templates are given with stitching lines and seam allowance cutting lines, so they can be used for any method of construction. Plan your project using the diagrams on pages 50 and 51 and then try your own hand at making this intriguing traditional pattern.

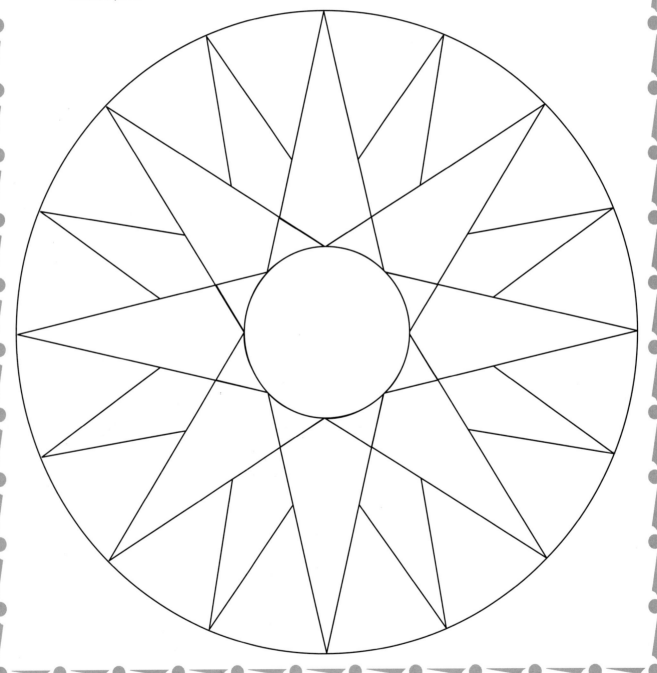

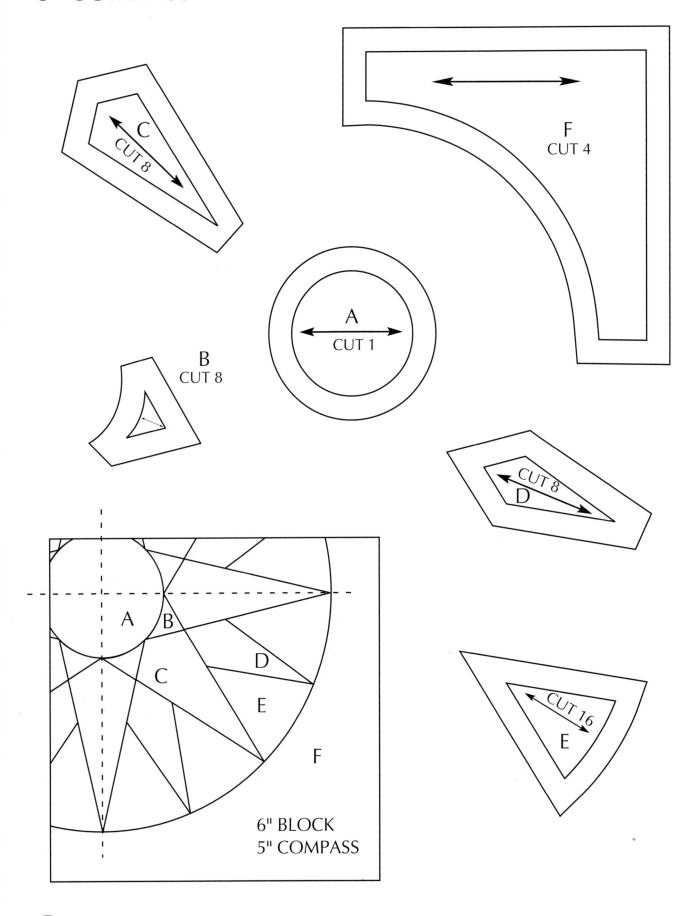

C
CUT 8

F
CUT 4

B
CUT 8

A
CUT 1

CUT 8
D

CUT 16
E

A B

C

D

E

F

6" BLOCK
5" COMPASS

Developing a Plan for Quilting
Yoshiko Kobayashi

*W*ith a complicated overall pieced design, planning the quilting can be as involved as planning the original design. To plan my quilting for "WWW Navigator's Compass," I made a photocopy of my scale drawing of the quilt's pieced design and drew in the proposed quilting patterns, using colored pencils (see below). You can't always follow such a plan exactly, but it gives you an idea how to proceed in such away that the quilting design will enhance the pieced patterns in your quilt.

Constructing a "Seamless" Compass Top
Ruth Cattles Cottrell

The construction detail that made me notice the Mariner's Compass quilt that inspired my quilt "Between the Devil and the Deep Blue Sea" was the fact that there were no seams in the areas between the Mariner's Compass blocks. In most Mariner's Compass quilts the compass design is pieced or appliquéd to a background square. These squares are then stitched together, and a secondary appliqué or quilting design is added in the seamed area. This quilt was not assembled that way. The cross seams lay directly under the center of each Compass, which means only an inch or two of the seam lines shows.

To achieve this look, you first appliqué each secondary appliqué block on large pieces of background fabric of a predetermined size (Fig. 1). You then sew these background pieces together and appliqué the compasses over the cross seams, between the secondary appliqué blocks (Fig. 2).

The only seams showing on the front of the quilt appear where the compasses almost touch and are only about 1" in length (Fig. 3).

Fig. 1
Cut large squares of the background fabric, using your overall quilt plan as a guide for measurements. Then stitch the secondary appliqué shape(s) to the center of each of these squares.

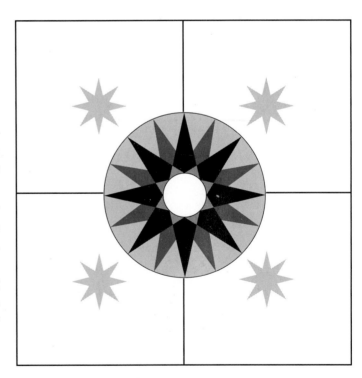

Fig. 2
Stitch the background squares together. Where seams intersect, appliqué a Mariner's Compass block, centering it over the intersecting seams.

$\mathcal{W}$hen making your compasses, it is important that the colors you choose for your points vary in color value (lightness and darkness). If you place points of the same value together, the pattern will disappear when viewed at a distance. To judge the values, I always view my fabric selections through a red filter before making my final decision. These plastic filters are available at quilt stores, but a clear red plastic notebook cover works just as well.

When I first selected fabric for this quilt I chose a darker brown for the small outside points. When I viewed it in conjunction with the dark blue, I realized it read the same degree of darkness, so I used the light brown batik instead.

By using different values in the compass, you ensure that your finished block will appear to have depth and will almost ripple or move when viewed.

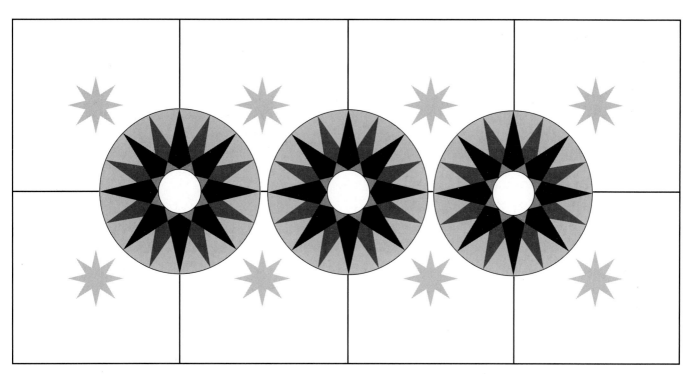

Fig. 3
Continue adding Mariner's Compass blocks until every intersecting seam is covered.

Using Block Segments & Broderie Perse
Corinne Appleton

Sense of Direction
Corinne Appleton, 1997
23" x 23"

After completing "IntergalactiCat," I dared to venture into the world of the Mariner's Compass once again. A sketch on a paper napkin provided the design impetus and the many hours spent doing broderie perse appliqué on a guild fundraising quilt had me itching to stitch in that style. The result was the finished quilt shown on page 64. A few tips on using block segments & broderie perse in your work follow:

•Generally, any time you halve or divide in any way a block or pattern, the segment must be drafted and constructed as a unique unit. Simply cutting apart a whole unit to create two halves will not work because the new units will be missing seam allowance.

The four star halves surrounding the central star in "IntergalactiCat" were made following this rule. The two outer half rays of "Sense of Direction" were re-made after forgetting this rule!

•Consider the above-mentioned fact when cutting out broderie perse motifs. Two half images will always need to be cut from two whole images anywhere there is a seam allowance needed.

•Don't worry if your broderie perse motifs are not quite symmetrical; not-quite-matched images can add interest. Taking that one step further, in "Sense of Direction" the second and third of the three roses contained within two compass rays were intentionally rotated slightly to add subtle variety.

•Use your imagination and your broderie perse fabric to make more from less. Take a second look at your fabric and you'll likely see opportunities to "build" design elements. The large flower in the corner of "Sense of Direction" is comprised of a number of pieces from the base fabric, appliquéd to one another before the outermost edge was appliquéd to the quilt top. Fill in any blanks with another composition and you have the added benefit of improved perspective and originality. Also, consider expanding your options by altering your cut-out motif – the tulip in the upper right corner was appliquéd to its green background, which was then reverse appliquéd to fit the center opening.

•Do as I say, not as I did. If you choose to work with a directional fabric or one from which you will be isolating design motifs, buy generously!

•Finally, I like to think that my attitude approaching the construction of "Sense of Direction" had something to do with its success. If you look carefully, it just might be the same force that brought "IntergalactiCat" to fruition – a certain cat-itude!

Preparing Templates for a Design
Gene P.H. Ives

To develop templates for a complicated design, I decide on the finished size, tape together blank newsprint paper to reach this size, and tape the paper to a blank wall. For my contest quilt, I sketched in the two mariners full size and then drafted a 16-point Mariner's Compass on top of the drawing of the mariners, to fill up the entire space.

I then went over all of the pencil lines with a magic marker, and numbered each piece of the picture. This is very important as this becomes my reference guide. The whole picture is then traced on freezer paper, and each piece is given the same number as on the original. Next I cut apart the freezer paper pieces (keeping my original drawing intact) and iron the paper pieces to selected fabrics. I cut the pieces out, adding ¼" seam allowances around each pattern piece. Then the pieces are sewn together – it's rather like building a puzzle.

Keeping everything organized as you sew a complicated design together can be a challenge. To help with this, I mark each piece with a plus sign indicating the horizontal and vertical lines so as to place each pattern piece on the straight of the grain of the fabric. To make piecing a little easier, I also draw little lines or hatch marks crossing over the outside dimensions of each piece so that these can then become reference points in joining the pieces (Fig. 1). They're used as notches are in dressmaking.

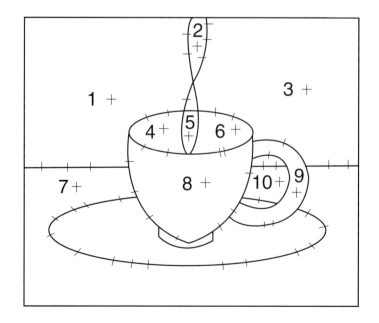

Fig. 1
Pattern drawn with plus signs indicating grain directions and hatch marks that can be transferred to the fabric pieces and used like notches for aligning pieces when they are sewn together.

Crossing the Bar
Gene P. H. Ives
56" x 56"

Using Large-Scale Floral Prints
Nancy Lambert

$\mathcal{I}$ use large-scale prints, especially large-scale florals to give added dimension to my quilt designs. I like the surface to be bright and show a lot of movement. Often solids or tone-on-tone prints give a very flat look to the quilt surface. I wanted to create depth and add interest to my Mariner's Compass quilt through large prints.

I tend to gravitate toward the large floral prints because a flower will often have many shades of one or several colors. If there is a pink rose in the print, there will be parts that are light pink or neutral, and parts that are dark pink or perhaps red. In one piece I can get the several shades needed to create depth.

To use such fabrics, I make a window template out of cardboard or something that is not transparent.

I want the template to block out the surrounding fabric so I only see the piece that is the template shape (Fig.1).

Once I find the portion of the fabric I want to use, I cut out a piece which is two or three inches bigger than the area I want to use. I then starch just the back of this fabric, to stabilize it. Because these pieces are cut on the bias for visual effects rather than grain line, the grain will be going in different directions for each, which means they can stretch and distort quite easily if not heavily starched.

I take the starched piece, mark the template outline on the back, and cut the shape out, adding seam allowance. I find that roughly cutting a large piece first and then marking and cutting the actual shape works very well.

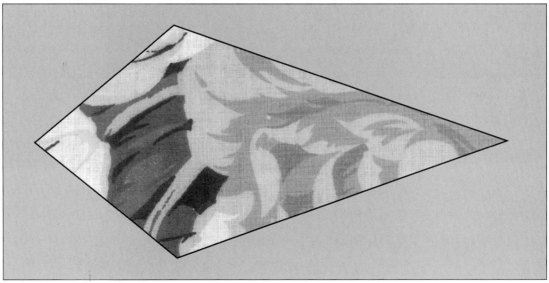

Fig. 1
Window template for cutting pieces from large-print florals, with print area to be used showing.

Star Flower
Nancy Lambert
51" x 51"

Developing a Complicated Design
Suzi Thomas McPherson
and
Brenda Smallwood Horton

The designs for the Mariner's Compass and lighthouse/rocks/sea areas were drawn first on 8½" x 11" typing paper. I find it much easier to make a small scale drawing to be enlarged than to begin working at full-scale. These drawings were taken to a copying business for enlargement.

I had calculated the percent enlargement needed (finished size divided by drawing size), and the copy shop produced the enlarged design in several sections. In the case of the Mariner's Compass area, it took eight 18" x 24" sheets, which were then fitted together like a puzzle and glued.

The next step came in taking long strips of paper from a roll and gluing them together to the approximate size of the finished quilt. The enlarged drawings of different design areas were placed on the background paper and moved around until the arrangement was pleasing. The drawings were affixed to the background paper using rubber cement, to allow readjustment when necessary. This also permits extra overlapped paper on the back to be easily peeled off and cut away.

The left side of the Mariner's Compass needed to be extended as if the points were reaching toward the sea and rocks, so another layer of paper was rubber cemented to that section, and the new points were drawn on it.

The moon/planet was drawn and again moved around on the master plan until the placement was right before cementing it down. Additional detail lines were added to the sea, transition area, and sky, as well as piecing lines for the Mariner's Compass.

The master plan was reversed and taped to a large picture window. Long strips of freezer paper were overlapped slightly and fused by tapping the point of a hot iron along the seams. The freezer paper was then taped over the master plan with the paper side (non-shiny side) out, and the entire drawing was traced onto the freezer paper. Sections of the Mariner's Compass oval, sky, rocks, and sea were cut apart to be worked separately.

The Mariner's Compass was machine pieced using the freezer paper as a foundation. The freezer paper aids in keeping seams flat because the fabric adheres to the plastic side when pressed.

The master plan was tacked to the front of a bookcase in the studio for easy reference during the entire construction process.

Charting Courses through Time
Suzi Thomas McPherson and Brenda Smallwood Horton
56" x 69"

The sky sections were marked with arrows to show which edges would be turned under for appliqué, which was a very helpful reference while basting edges of the individual pieces. Arrows were also drawn on the rock pieces to illustrate the direction of the fabric when using stripes and plaids. The original small drawings also served as references at this stage (Fig. 1).

The fabrics for the rocks and sea were arranged from lightest to darkest, then numbered (placing a piece of numbered masking tape in the corner of each fabric chunk). The sections on the small drawings were numbered to correspond to the lightness or darkness wanted in that area. These numbers were then transferred to the freezer paper drawing before cutting it apart into individual pieces. Because the sea pieces were so numerous and similar,

these pieces were also labeled with letters on the freezer paper and master plan to easily locate the exact piece needed. Snips of fabric choices were taped to the Mariner's Compass drawing (Fig. 2). Purple ray points were lettered to indicate depth of color. The numbers on the compass relate to stitching order and placement as the points are a variety of sizes.

The freezer paper was now cut into individual pieces and ironed onto the correct fabric. The pieces were hand basted with appropriate edges tuned under, then hand appliquéd to each other in sections.

Organza overlays were basted over the sky fabric pieces, which already had the freezer paper ironed on. Fullness was eased into the organza to give a three-dimensional effect, but we discovered that much of that fullness dis-

Fig. 1

Original sketch for the lighthouse/rocks/sea area. Numbers refer to the fabrics to be used for each area.

peared during the construction and More fullness should be added when this technique is tried again. The sky pieces were planned to overlap onto the organza pieces for appliqué. Cording in the sea floor section was basted onto the piece to be overlapped. The folded-under edge of the top piece could then be appliquéd easily along the stitching line of the cording.

The Mariner's Compass section was appliquéd onto the sky section. The rock/sea section was appliquéd onto this section. The ocean floor with fossil fabric section was added last.

Quilting lines in the sky followed the planned current-swirls of the appliqué with additional quilting lines added in the flowing style. These quilting lines intentionally crossed the appliqué line from the Mariner's Compass section to distract from the hard oval edge and continue the flow of the currents behind the star.

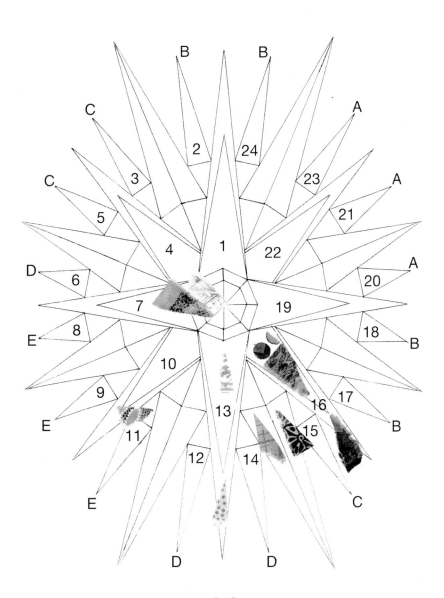

Fig. 2

Original sketch for the Mariner's Compass area, with several fabric pieces attached to indicate fabric plans.

Looking for Inspiration

Developing the design idea for "Ancient Mariner: The Purple Empire"

Mary L. Hackett

If I am lucky, inspiration and hard work come together and put me on the road to a very satisfying conclusion – a quilt with a voice that speaks to viewers. Working on "Ancient Mariner: The Purple Empire" was a joy, and it is my hope the quilt will speak to others.

The Phoenicians occupied various lands surrounding the Mediterranean Sea from the sixteenth century B.C. until 65 B.C., when Phoenicia's status as a separate country was terminated because the Romans added it to the province of Syria.

The Phoenicians, a Semitic people, are considered to have introduced glass to the Egyptians, the alphabet to the Greeks, and purple textiles to the world at large. They not only sailed to Britain, but also circumnavigated Africa. From their city-state of Tyre, they founded Carthage, Utica, Gades, and other cities as trading posts, and influenced the entire known world with their culture. All this I discovered, or rather rediscovered, because of the MAQS "New Quilts from Old Favorites" competition.

Not one to repeat a component of a quilt once if I can help it, let alone a dozen or more times for a traditional bed quilt, I had no intention of entering this contest when I initially heard of it. But my work and my life have always been grounded in the love of words, and the name of this block – Mariner's Compass – intrigued me. I began writing down words and phrases that came to mind when thinking of this block.

I looked up "compass" in the dictionary. "An instrument for determining directions," Webster said. "The enclosing line or limits of any area, measurement round. Space within limits; area; extent; range; scope. Due or proper limits; moderate bounds." Moderate? Not me. "An instrument for describing circles. To extend or stretch around." Hmm. "To attain or achieve; accomplish; obtain, contrive, or scheme." Maybe.

How about "mariner?" "One who directs or assists in the navigation of a ship; seaman; sailor." No surprises there.

I began to fantasize about the various images the words brought to mind, and let my mind roam over the sea, into the heavens, and back into history. The phrase "ancient mariner" kept coming to mind, though I did not wish to revisit "The Rime of the Ancient Mariner" and its hero's albatross. I was thinking more of the idea that the Mariner's Compass quilt block was so named because of its circular shape and perhaps historical ties to old maps, signs of stars, and the longings of the home-bound wives of seafarers as they pieced familiar motifs into their quilts.

Who, I wondered, would be a really ancient mariner? The Phoenicians, I had been taught in school, were the first to develop a number of innovations in sailing vessels and navigation. Their travels impacted peoples around the Mediterranean, I remembered, but exactly how?

Ancient Mariner: The Purple Empire
Mary L. Hackett
58" x 75"

As I found reference materials describing the ancient Phoenicians, I became more and more excited by the impact these people had, not only economically, but also on the art, culture, literature, and ultimately the progress of mankind. There was ample material illustrating the pottery, metalwork, glass, and dyestuffs produced by Phoenician craftsmen and artisans, and evidence that theirs was the first written language system introduced to the Greeks, facilitating the development of Greek literature and philosophy. In fact, had the world been without the influence of these "ancient mariners," much of what we know as civilization would have been delayed or would never have existed. If this quilter needed further fodder for the launching of a Mariner's Compass quilt based on the Phoenicians, the fact that they developed Tyrian purple dye from the murex snail and marketed it around the Mediterranean clinched the decision.

Armed with the many photographic references of sculpture, pottery, glassware, and carved images, I began drawing my mariner.

I pictured him seated, marveling at a globe or disk in his lap, the physical manifestation of an idea: a method of traveling across the sea, trading his wares, and establishing his culture at trading posts in far-flung locations.

And to support the image of the power this ability had to transform the known world, I designed a setting for him which incorporated the glassware, textiles, written language, and symbolism of this culture. His ship, seen through the window, is silhouetted against the twilight horizon. He wears

the purple robes which became the sign of wealth, power, and authority throughout subsequent history. And at his feet stands a vessel of glass, formed from a very plentiful resource in the Mediterranean – sand.

The methods I used to construct this quilt are no different than those employed by many other quilters. I have used nearly life-size figures in at least two other significant pieces. My means of transferring images, making patterns, choosing and sewing cloth, and quilting the piece, are taught in classes or lectures of others.

But just as I searched for the idea that would spark my imagination and carry me through the process, the inspiration for any quilter's next quilt is wholly within that quilter. Consider the search for inspiration as part of the process – definable, concrete, a skill you can learn by practice. And you know what practice can do for you!

Adding Photocopy Transfers to Quilts
Jo Anna Johnson

Technology can offer great tools for artists. Caryl Bryer Fallert uses her computer to create designs and then to manipulate them in various ways. She even uses it to try a variety of colors to see which will be the most affective in her finished quilt. I used the program Adobe Photoshop™ to join together two images into a third for the central image of my quilt, "Which Way?" Photocopying is another technology quilt artists can use.

I used the photocopy transfer process to apply historical images to my quilt. This technique is easy to do and will successfully transfer any image that can be photocopied. Photocopy transfers were especially appropriate for "Which Way?" because of its historical perspective. I wanted the viewer to better understand and remember African American and white relations through visual images of the past as well as the related words and phrases.

I found these images in the Special Collections at Southern Illinois University at Carbondale's Morris Library. The images came from several of their collections including Civil War broadsides, the Jan Roddy collection, the Katherine Dunham Papers, and the Cairo – Racial Problems Collection. They were found by using a card catalog in the Special Collections area. My quilt includes everything from images from photographs of racial unrest in Cairo, Illinois, in the late 1960's to graphic art from pamphlets Katherine Dunham collected. I even found a few illustrations in a 1970 Senior Thesis, The Anti-Slavery Movement in Randolph County, Illinois, by Dora M. Spinney.

You don't have to use historical images. Anything that is not copyright restricted and can be photocopied will work, but the images that work best are those of high contrast. Often photographs are too dark or too light. If you have a dark image, be sure to use a light background. Line drawings and graphic prints work very well because of their high contrast. You can create your own drawings or text, but remember the image will be reversed.

To solve this problem, I made a photocopy transparency (as you would make for using with an overhead projector) and then turned it over and copied it again on paper, backwards. There is more than one way to transfer photocopies on to fabric. I chose this method for its ease and because it does not leave a plastic-like film coating. The fabric is as soft when you complete the transfer as when you began the process.

Which Way?

JoAnna Johnson
68" x 68"

Supplies Needed for Photocopy Transfer Process:

- Photocopies
- 100% cotton fabric, washed, no starch or softener
- Freezer paper
- Plate glass, a little larger than you largest image
- Paint remover. Be sure to read the warnings on the can before proceeding.
- Iron
- Masking tape
- Scissors
- Foam core, four inches larger than your glass
- T-pins
- Old metal tablespoon and glass dish, not to be used for food again

Steps in the Photocopy Transfer Process

1. Prepare the fabric.

Trace on your yardage pattern pieces for the shapes that will contain the photocopied images, leaving plenty of room between shapes for seam allowances.

2. Position the fabric over the piece of plate glass and the foam core.

Lay down your foam core piece onto a flat surface, then lay the glass on top of the foam core. Center the fabric over the glass, with its edges extending beyond it. Then insert pins through these edges and into the foam core, to hold the fabric in place. Use T-pins and angle them with the top of the T away from the glass.

3. Prepare the photocopy.

Make a freezer paper frame for the photocopy you want to transfer to fabric. If it's possible, have some white space around all edges of the image on the paper photocopy. This will make it easier to attach the freezer paper frame.

To prepare the frame, cut a piece of freezer paper two inches bigger than the photocopy. Cut out of the middle of the freezer paper a hole as big as the image to be transferred. You can trace the outline of your image on the shiny side of the freezer if you like, to provide you with a cutting line. Tape the photocopy to the freezer paper so the image is seen through the hole and faces the shiny side of the freezer paper.

4. Position the photocopy on the fabric.

Lay the paper photocopy of the image face down on the fabric and use masking tape to secure it to the fabric. Tape only the edges of the freezer paper frame.

5. Make the transfer.

Pour a small amont of paint remover into a dish. Take a spoonful from the dish, pour it onto the photocopy, and then rub the frosting-like chemical into the paper using the bowl of the spoon. You can also use the edge of the spoon to transfer; this will give a completely different look. Experiment. You may have to use additional paint remover for a very large image. The chemical releases the copier toner onto the fabric. The paint remover never touches the fabric. Fresh photocopies work best, but they are not necessary. You will rub for less than a minute before the image will be transferred. Then remove the paper by peeling it back from the fabric, scrape excess paint remover into the dish with the spoon and carefully dispose of the paper. Note: If you happen to get paint remover on your fabric wash it out immediately and thoroughly. Please read all warnings on the paint remover can before using it.

6. Set the image.

Use a dry iron on a cotton setting for about a minute to set. Even after it has been set, this image will fade when the fabric is washed and dried. It won't disappear even after several washings, but it will fade more with each. I recommend you use this process only when the fabric will not be washed.

This method not only works with black and white images, but also with color ones. It's a great way to tell a family's history. I'm sure you will think of many ways this technique will give your quilts a richer meaning.

Piecing Architectural Designs
Elsie Vredenburg

Quilters often want a building translated into fabric. Be it a photo of your house, a favorite historic landmark, or a landscape – it is possible to use a photo to create a drawing from which you can piece a fabric picture. With this method for piecing, you will only work with straight seams and a minimum of set-in corners, which can result in a somewhat angular interpretation of the photo. However, short, straight seams with the angles at close intervals can be made to "read" as curved lines.

Making the Pattern

For your first project using this method, select a photo that has simple lines and a minimum of detail and "clutter." As you become more proficient, you can add details and complexity.

Determine the size you want your picture to be. It can be a single block or the whole quilt. I have done pieced pictures ranging in size from 3½" x 3½" to 48" x 60". Sketch in the main elements (Fig. 1). There are several methods of enlarging: use an opaque projector; project a slide onto a large piece of paper and trace the design; enlarge using a grid; or draw freehand. Tracing paper is a good choice, although I often use freezer paper because it is larger and readily available. This drawing will become your master drawing, which will remain intact and serve as a guide for piecing the quilt.

Since only straight lines will be used for piecing, take a ruler and "straighten" all curved lines. The degree of complexity can be adjusted during this process. If you want to simplify the picture, use longer lines before changing directions (Fig. 2). For a more detailed picture, use shorter lines, changing direction more often and making more gradual changes (Fig. 3).

I prefer to avoid as many set-in corners as possible. For this it is necessary to divide the drawing into sections. Study the drawing carefully, trying to pick out natural divisions or major sections. It simplifies piecing if at least one seam goes all the way across the block or wallhanging, either horizontally or vertically, whichever is least distracting (Fig. 4). After determining the major divisions, work section by section, adding seam lines wherever necessary to facilitate piecing (Fig. 5, p. 82).

Fig. 1
Sketch of lighthouse.

Once you are satisfied with your drawing, darken all the lines with a fine marker. I find it helpful to lightly shade in design elements with a colored pencil so that I don't get confused later when I am selecting fabrics.

Turn the drawing over and tape it to the table. If you have a light table, it makes this step much easier. Tape a piece of freezer paper, dull side up, over the drawing. (For large pictures, you can either work in sections or tape two pieces of paper together.) Trace all lines onto the freezer paper, using a ruler to keep your lines straight as you trace. This drawing will be used for your templates, so it needs to be accurate. This drawing will be in reverse of the original.

Number each piece the same on both drawings. This is essential for putting the puzzle back together. Your pattern is now complete.

Selecting Fabrics

Fabric selection is a large part of what will make your quilt uniquely yours. Each of us has certain tastes in fabrics. Your fabric collection has its own character, and is a reflection of your personality.

You can be as exact as possible in replicating your photo, or as creative as you wish. When making pieced pictures, you learn to see fabrics in a new way. The more you do this, the easier it becomes. Some colors are obvious: sky is blue or gray, grass is green. But there are still choices: one fabric for a consistent look, or several fabrics for a pieced, scrappy look; cloudy or clear; night or day.

I rarely use solids; some people use

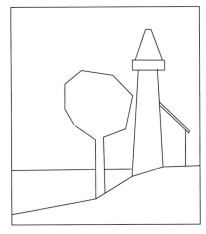

Fig. 2
Simple rendering of the design.

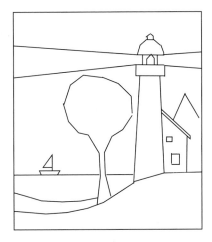

Fig. 3
More complex rendering of the design.

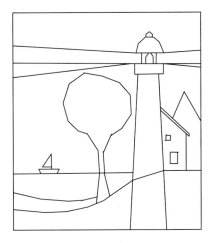

Fig. 4
All curved lines have been straightened and major sections have been determined.

all solids. Don't get hung up on choosing just the "right" fabric. There are probably lots of "right" choices. Relax.

Make your choice and get on with the project. You can change your mind right up to the moment of actually cutting the fabric, and even after the block is sewn if you don't mind ripping out!

For depth, use smaller, more grayed and indistinct prints in the distance, and brighter, larger prints in the foreground. I try to use prints which will camouflage seam lines, especially in the backgrounds. Avoid directional prints, except to emphasize design elements. For instance, I like to use plaids for windows, to give a suggestion of sashing.

Some very unlikely and even "ugly" fabrics may provide just the effect you wish to achieve. Some tropical prints have large areas of the design which have their own special qualities. Try to look at the fabric not as a whole, but with an open mind to the possibilities that just a small section of a print may offer.

Construction

Cut apart the reverse drawing, working with only one section at a time, to avoid confusion and loss of small pieces. These pieces will be your templates. Use a rotary cutter with an old blade for cutting these.

With a hot dry iron, press the freezer paper templates to the back of your fabric. Try to keep grain line consistent with the edge of the block; marking it on the template will help. With a ruler and rotary cutter, cut pieces out, adding a ¼" seam allowance.

The order of stitching will be in reverse of the order used in cutting the picture apart, starting with small inner pieces and adding pieces to "build" the design.

Sew pieces together by lining up the edges of the paper, and sewing along the edge. Do not remove the paper until you have sewn all the seams on the section.

Press with a dry iron. I usually try to press toward the design element that appears to be in the foreground; i.e. toward the tree rather than the sky.

For very small sections, I often piece right on the paper, using the "sew & flip" method. In fact, you can cut the pattern into sections and use the "sew & flip" method for an entire block if you prefer that method.

When you have finished piecing your block, or finished each section if it is a large piece, remove all paper, give it a good pressing, being careful not to stretch it out of shape, and square it up by trimming any uneven edges with a rotary cutter.

You are now ready to add a border or set it into a quilt.

Fig. 5
Completed drawing with all piecing lines added. Whenever possible, seam lines have been added at angles to avoid set-in corners.

82

Split Rock Sunset
Elsie Vredenburg
53" x 59"

Patterns & Instructions

When This You See, Remember Me
Judith Thompson
77" x 77"

Combining Old & New Blocks
Judith Thompson

I like antique fabrics and blocks. When I see them at shows, I find myself trying to visualize how they could be set to complete a quilt.

"When This You See, Remember Me" was inspired by antique blocks I purchased. I used the blocks as a guide for developing a pattern for constructing the additional blocks needed. In the process of working with this quilt, I discovered a few things about working with these older elements.

•Fabrics in the blocks may be brittle or badly worn. If you feel you need to make some repairs, make them with fabric from same era and be sure to do that before the blocks are sewn together and quilted. Some quilters use reproduction fabrics, but I try not to do that. Sometimes I will sacrifice a poor quality block in a set and use its good fabrics for repairs in other blocks. Be sure to avoid fusibles!

•Piecing by hand is less stressful on old fabrics.

•During quilting, "tender spots" may need to be stitched through one stitch at a time, to avoid unnecessary manipulation of brittle fabrics.

•Many old blocks are of a distorted size, which may be a reason why the original quilter never used them in a quilt! You will need to square up blocks before setting them together. If you are creating new blocks to be integrated with them, you will need to survey the varying sizes, "averaging" them to come up with something that will integrate with the entire set.

•Many old fabrics bleed. Be sure to test for colorfastness if you plan to wash the quilt.

The pattern I developed for the four blocks I added to the corners of my quilt follows (p. 86), with indications of the number of pieces to cut for each block.

Fig. 1

The signature blocks in "When This You See, Remember Me" include inscriptions as noted in this diagram. The four corner blocks are new blocks made in the same design as the antique blocks, and inscribed as indicated.

Judith Thompson	M.L. Hinkle	M. Hoffman	When This You See, Remember Me
Elizabeth Levering	Peter Hinkle Sr.	Margaret Hinkle	Amanda Hinkle
Sarah McGomley	Susan Hinkle	W.H. Levering	Marian Levering
Wenonah, NJ	JA Levering	J. H. Hoffman	1996

FULL-SIZE PATTERNS
14" Block

A
CUT 1
white

E
CUT 12
white

B
CUT 6
red

C
CUT 6
red

D
CUT 6
white

Appliqué templates, also used as quilting templates

Drafting "Free-Style" Compass Blocks
Debbie Hern

Drafting "free-style" Mariner's Compass blocks is easy. In fact, it's easier than drafting traditional Mariner's Compass designs because there's less measuring involved. You don't need a degree in engineering! What you do need are a few supplies: paper, a ruler or straight-edge, and a compass. If you plan on drafting many Mariner's Compass blocks, go to an art supply store and buy a fairly good compass. You want one with arms that stay put once you have them adjusted to the proper measurement.

On paper, use your compass to draw a circle the desired size of your compass block. To do this, decide what diameter block you wish to make and adjust your compass until the arms are apart exactly half of that measurement. My Mariner's Compass blocks are 12" in diameter, so I positioned the arms of my compass exactly 6" apart (the radius of a 12" circle).

Then anywhere within that circle, draw another smaller circle. It can be a concentric circle, with its center point the same as that of the larger circle, or one that is off-center. It can be large or small. In between these two circles is where you will draw the "rays" of your compass. Draw in the rays wherever you like. You can make them skinny or fat – whatever pleases you (Fig. 1). I usually sketch them in lightly with my pencil first, until I think they look right,

then I make a more definite line with a ruler and my pencil. You wouldn't want seam lines that weren't perfectly straight.

The points of each ray usually touch the outer circle, but they don't have to. If you want points that "float," you can certainly design it that way. But you'll have to elongate one of the ray's sides out to the outer circle, because there will have to be a seam there at that point when you piece the block. At the base of your rays, the lines you draw can meet exactly or overlap each other. If they cross or overlap each other, you'll have created another pattern piece.

I use foundation piecing for constructing Mariner's Compass blocks. This involves making a paper drawing or pattern to which fabric pieces are stitched, one by one. The paper is later removed from the back.

To prepare your drawing for foundation piecing, cut the large circle out on the solid line, and then the smaller circle out of the center, as shown in Fig. 2. Save this center circle to use as a pattern piece for the center of your block. If you've drafted a compass where all of the rays intersect at their points with the outer circle and at their base with the inner circle (i.e. no floating points or overlapping rays), just cut along one of the lines of one of the rays and begin foundation piecing at this point.

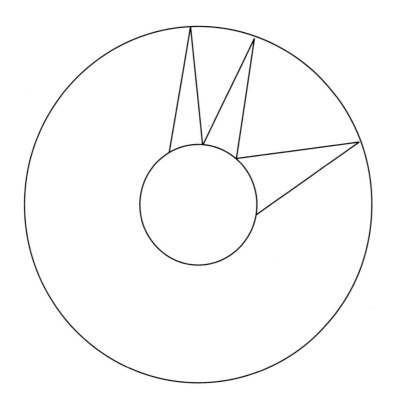

Fig. 1

Two concentric circles have been drawn and rays are being added between the two circles.

Broken lines show where to cut fabric.
Solid lines indicate where to stitch.

Begin
foundation piecing
at this
point. (Add a ¼"
seam allowance
here, too.)

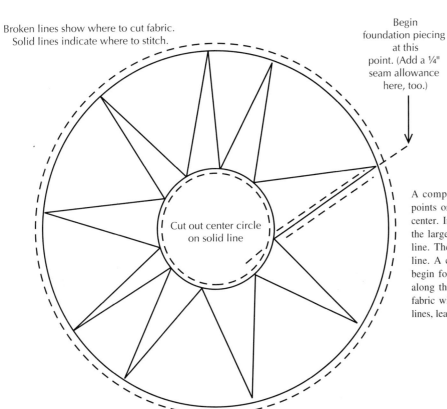

Cut out center circle
on solid line

Fig. 2

A compass design drawn with no floating points or overlapping rays, and a concentric center. In preparation for foundation piecing, the large circle is being cut out on the solid line. The center is also cut out on the solid line. A cut has been made along one ray to begin foundation piecing. Fabric will be left along these edges and the circle edges. The fabric will later be trimmed along the broken lines, leaving ¼" extra for seam allowance.

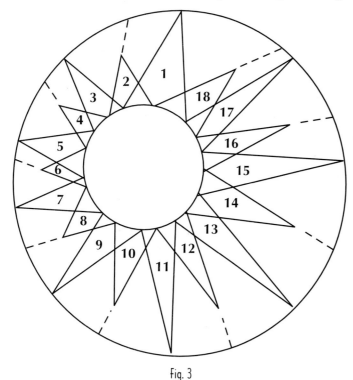

Fig. 3

A compass design with overlapping rays and some floating points. Dotted lines indicate where the pattern would need to be cut into units for foundation piecing.

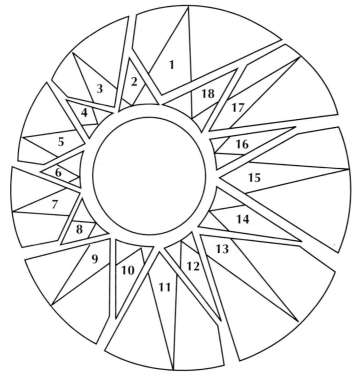

Fig. 4

The same design as Fig. 3 exploded to show the separate units. Numbers indicate the order in which the units would be assembled after each was foundation pieced. Prior to assembling units, the fabric edges of each unit are trimmed to ¼" from the edge of the paper foundation, to add seam allowance.

If you've designed a compass with intersecting lines or points that float, it will not be possible to foundation piece the block without cutting the paper pattern into smaller units. It's a very good idea to number the rays or units of your pattern in sequence around the block. Then you'll be able to sew them back together in the proper order (Figs. 3, 4). Use the small circle center as a pattern for a center circle, adding ¼" allowance.

To prepare for foundation piecing, cut the paper pattern where necessary, foundation piece each unit individually, then sew them all together in the proper order around the block. This is where it will help if you've numbered the rays.

Don't forget to add a ¼" fabric seam allowance around each pattern piece and around the entire block when you trim your fabrics! And remember that if you use freezer paper for foundation piecing and you draft your design on the dull, paper side and sew on the shiny side, your sewn block will be the reverse or mirror image of your drawing. This may or may not matter to you. Appliqué the small circle in place last.

There are many good books available on foundation piecing if you need help with that technique, one of which is Firm Foundations by Jane Hall and Dixie Haywood (AQS). Two tips which I found very helpful in my own foundation piecing: use small stitches in your seams so that when it's time to remove the paper, it will be well perforated. The more perforations, the easier the paper will be to remove. And, don't use a steam iron setting when you press. Steam will cause the paper to buckle and shrink.

Cosmosis
Debbie Hern
72" x 72"

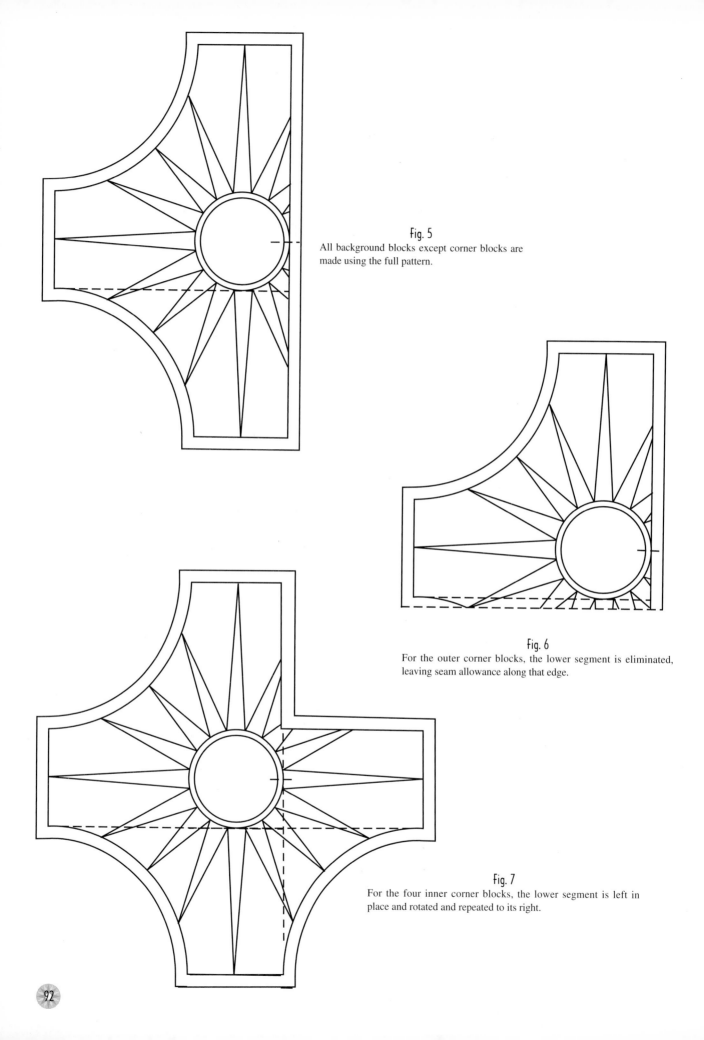

Fig. 5
All background blocks except corner blocks are
made using the full pattern.

Fig. 6
For the outer corner blocks, the lower segment is eliminated,
leaving seam allowance along that edge.

Fig. 7
For the four inner corner blocks, the lower segment is left in
place and rotated and repeated to its right.

1. First make the background Compass blocks. Using the pattern provided on page 94, make 24 background Mariner's Compass blocks. Sixteen of these blocks are exactly the pattern outline shape (Fig. 5), four of them (for the outer corners) have a piece cut off from one side (Fig. 6), and four of them (for the inside corners) have the same piece added to another side (Fig. 7). In my quilt there are two variations for the design of this block. I've provided the pattern for one of them. Or you can draft your own (even a "free-style" design), using the outline of the pattern.

2. Sew or appliqué a 4" compass or circle of fabric to the center of each background compass. If you are going to add compasses, draft and sew 24 four-inch diameter "free-style" Mariner's Compass blocks for the center of each background block. My 4" compass blocks also have moon shapes appliquéd in the center circles.

3. Sew together all 24 background blocks as shown in the diagram. Leave a 23½" (24" finished size) square opening in the center of the quilt top.

4. Draft and sew 12, twelve-inch diameter "free-style" Mariner's Compass blocks.

5. Sew or appliqué the 12, twelve inch compass blocks into the circle openings between the background blocks.

6. For the center compass, start by drawing a 24" square on a large piece of paper (or two pieces of freezer paper taped together). Inside this 24" square, draft a Mariner's Compass, either "freestyle" or traditional, centered or off-centered. Mine has a 9" circle centered in the 24" square and rays of varying sizes and lengths. But they are evenly spaced around the center. (I had to measure around the center circle for this.)

If you want some of the rays of your compass to extend beyond the 24" square, as some of mine do, draw them to do so on the paper pattern.

Using your paper pattern, piece the center compass into a 24½" square (24" finished size) which will fit into the center opening of your quilt top.

If you've made some of the rays of your compass extend beyond the 24" center square, you will have to reverse appliqué them so that these points will show. When you piece the 24" square center into place, stop wherever you run into one of these longer rays and knot off at this point. Then begin your seam again on the other side of the ray and continue on around the square.

When you've finished sewing the center into place, carefully cut the quilt top above each of your longer rays starting at the center of each ray and continuing to cut down the middle of the ray almost to the point. It helps if you first baste the ray into place under the quilt top. Now turn the raw edges of the quilt top under to the edge of the compass ray all the way around to fully expose the ray. Appliqué the quilt top to the ray right at the outer edge of the ray. This is a bit tricky, especially at the point of the ray, since there won't be much seam allowance. Patience is required!

7. For a scalloped edge like mine, each scallop's finished diameter is exactly 4¼".

Pattern for Background Blocks
"Cosmosis"
Shown at 50% actual size.
Seam allowance included where indicated.

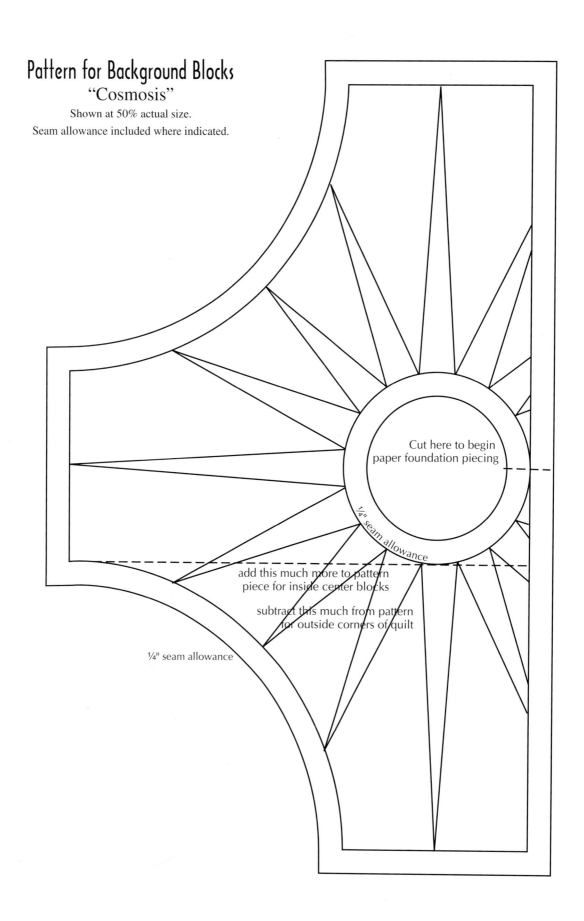

Cut here to begin
paper foundation piecing

¼" seam allowance

add this much more to pattern
piece for inside center blocks

subtract this much from pattern
for outside corners of quilt

¼" seam allowance

Compass Sunflowers & Patterns
Sylvia A. Whitesides

*M*y design was based on Vincent Van Gogh's painting titled, Still Life with Sunflowers. *Once I had imagined creating its sunflowers using the Mariner's Compass design, I tried piecing a few and then created the master plan shown.*

Using the master plan, I gathered and prepared fabrics, hand-dyeing the yellow background fabric and many others, and combining these fabrics with commercial printed fabric. By using many shades of golds, yellows, browns, oranges, and reds, I achieved the feeling of exuberance of real sunflowers and the Van Gogh painting. In all, I tie-dyed 15 yards of bleached muslin with fiber reactive dyes.

Positioning templates carefully, I was able to make the Mariner's Compass blocks look like sunflowers. I found the colors worked best when they radiated light to dark from the center of the sunflower out, or had high contrast between points and background.

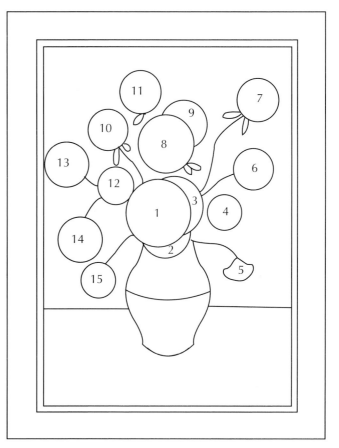

Master Plan

Fig 1. (detail of "Sunflowers after Vincent," Block 10)
Many of the sunflower centers have fabrics that have dotted textures, which gives the effect of the seeds in real sunflowers. I also used free-motion machine quilting to highlight some of the sunflower centers and leaves, to give the effect of texture.

Flower #5

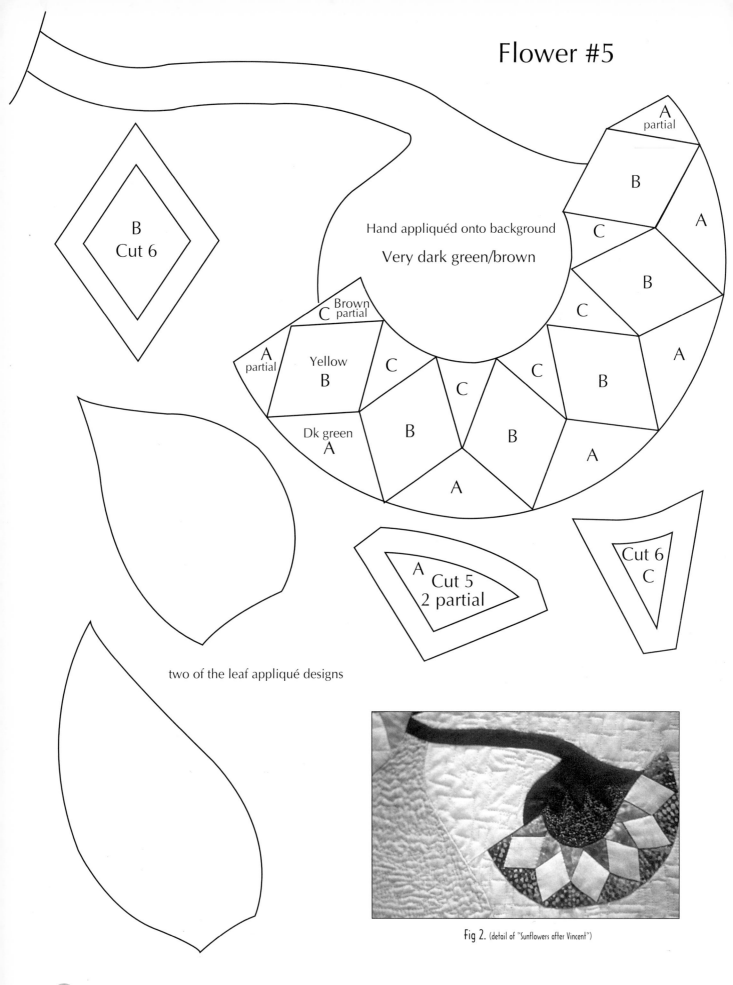

B
Cut 6

Hand appliquéd onto background

Very dark green/brown

A partial

B

C

A

B

C

A

C Brown partial

A partial

Yellow B

C

C

B

Dk green A

B

C

B

A

A

B

A

two of the leaf appliqué designs

A Cut 5 2 partial

Cut 6 C

Fig 2. (detail of "Sunflowers after Vincent")

96

Sunflowers after Vincent
Sylvia A. Whitesides
51" x 65"

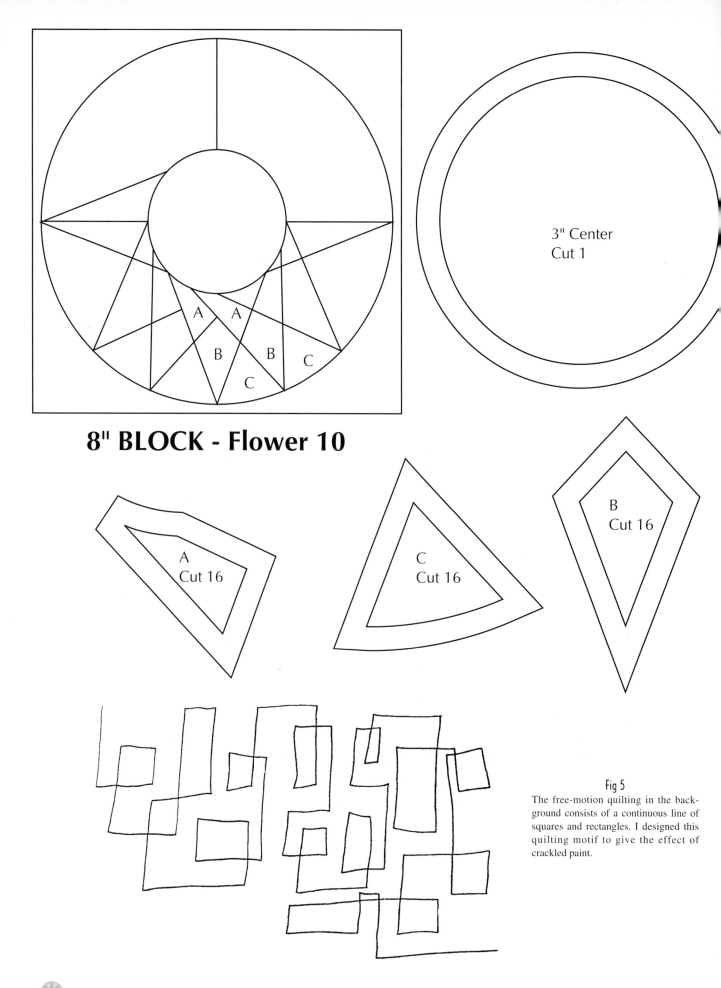

3" Center
Cut 1

8" BLOCK - Flower 10

A
Cut 16

C
Cut 16

B
Cut 16

Fig 5
The free-motion quilting in the background consists of a continuous line of squares and rectangles. I designed this quilting motif to give the effect of crackled paint.

Making "Homeward Bound"
Janet Duncan Dignan

*O*ne of the rules for this contest stated "the quilt must be an interpretation of the Mariner's Compass pattern and should be recognizable in some way as related to the Mariner's Compass." I decided my Mariner's Compass would be recognizable!

When drafting the Mariner's Compass pattern, the best rules I found to follow are in Judy Mathieson's book-Mariner's Compass Quilts, New Directions. Draft one or two 6" compasses following her precise directions. You will then feel more confident and knowledgeable.

Drafting:

Draw one quarter of a 32 ray compass measuring 12" from center to tip of largest ray. Draw sewing lines on both sides of each ray:

• *2 major halves* – draw six sewing lines angled from center line to edge (Fig 1)

• *1 second largest* – draw four sewing lines angled from center line to edge

• *2 medium* – draw three sewing lines angled from center line to edge

• *4 small* – draw three sewing lines angled from center line to edge

Have your local photo copy shop double this in size and print five copies. (One extra – just in case!) You can now build a 48" diameter Mariner's Compass with 32 rays.

Fabric:

Get out the fabric stash! Organize by color and arrange each color group from light to dark to create a controlled palette.

• *4 major rays* – bright, clear

• *4 second largest* – soft, light

• *8 medium* – cool, dull

• *16 small* – rich, deep, dark

• *The tip of each ray is the same fabric on both sides.*

As you move around the compass (i.e. yellow, orange, pink, red, etc.) introduce bits of the next color to the right side of the ray. For the pie-shaped background pieces, select a non-directional deep blue that will blend with the bargello sky. As you cut out each paper pie piece, use three dabs of a glue stick to hold it to fabric. Cut fabric, being sure to include a ¼" seam allowance.

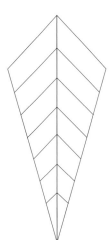

Fig 1

Sewing lines for piecing both sides of a ray.

Sky:

Bargello style. Cut six 4½" strips of five deep blue fabrics and sew together in sets of five for easy handling. Press to one side. Cut across in 2" strips. Join four strips lengthwise for width of sky. Continue to build these strips up alternating one half rectangle right for five rows then left for four rows. Continue in this manner, piecing rows from sea level up, adding 2" strips of muslin in the area that will be behind the Compass and eventually cut away.

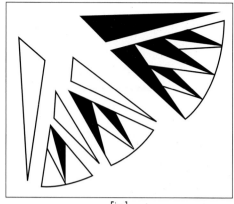

Fig 1

Compass:

Cut out one half of a major ray. Starting at top, place two fabric pieces right sides together on unlined side of paper, making sure each piece will be larger than the pattern section it is to cover plus seam allowance. Starting at least ¼" outside the paper, machine stitch on the line going at least ¼" beyond the paper. Fold second piece down, press firmly, cut to ¼". Continue this system down to the point. Each half ray is built in this manner. Join sections for ⅛ of the compass at a time, in the order illustrated using the following machine appliqué technique.

Machine Appliqué:

Spray about a teaspoon of spray starch into a saucer and with a small art paint brush, moisten center seam allowance on one side of a ray. Fold to back and press. Using a light box, place pressed edge over seam allowance of companion piece matching as necessary and pin. Machine appliqué the seam using extra small zigzag stitch, invisible thread on top and regular thread in bobbin.

Sea:

Five rows of 3" fabric, three greens in each row, cut at 45° angles with the brightest fabric at the horizon.

Earth:

On a 15" x 70" length of tracing paper, draw vertical lines at 60° angles. Machine stitch assorted earthtone browns from center to outside edges.

Trees:

Cut a number of dark green fabrics in strips 1", 1½", 2", 2½" widths. Using a center triangle base 1½" x 3¼", machine stitch strips at random on alternate sides of triangle making each tree layer or row. The smallest tree is one row, the largest six. Machine appliqué trees to quilt as previously described.

Stars:

Make thirteen 6" two-tone Mariner's Compasses and machine appliqué in position as shown in photograph. At the local nature shop I purchased a planisphere to help with star locations. A good friend, a retired Naval officer, advised me in the selection of stars used in navigation, artistic license notwithstanding! Cut out sections of fabric behind Mariner's Compass, trees, and stars. Remove all paper from the project, pulling gently at seams. Tweezers will come in very handy!

Finishing Up:

Layer your quilt with batting and pin baste. Machine quilt the Mariner's Compass with various 30 weight thread to match or contrast the rays using a lengthened stitch and a walking foot. The sky, sea, earth and trees are quilted free motion with 60 weight embroidery threads. Make a deep blue bias strip 2" x 23" and bind your quilt in the usual manner.

Best Hint:

Use surgical gloves when free-motion sewing. Incredible how they ease the process of moving about a large, bulky project.

Homeward Bound
Janet Duncan Dignan
63" x 76"

Making an Earth Angel

Mary Jo Dalrymple
and
Paulette Peters

Finished size for each angel quilt: 20" wide x 23" long

(block size: 20" x 20", plus 3" border lower edge)

Since the construction of this design can be a bit challenging, we recommend previous experience with the Mariner's Compass. Some seam allowances need to be left free. Be sure to think ahead.

Fabric selection:

Look for colors, values, and even a fabric design itself which convey your angel's theme. Try to include meaning on every level. For example, use a floral print for a floral angel, rather than settling for a geometric or plain fabric. Don't be too fast to sew the pieces together. Take time to find just the right fabric which will make your piece sing the song you hear in your imagination. You may even want to put the pieces you are happy with on a square of flannel, roll everything up and take it with you to the quilt shop. For various angels we sometimes divided or combined templates. Be flexible.

Cutting:

Cut the fabric pieces needed for an angel, cutting the number of pieces indicated on the templates. Be sure to reverse templates as needed. Be sure to add seam allowances to each template as you cut it out.

Assembly:

We used machine piecing, but this is a good project for hand piecing. As in hand piecing, we did not cross over the seam allowances, but lock-stitched at each junction.

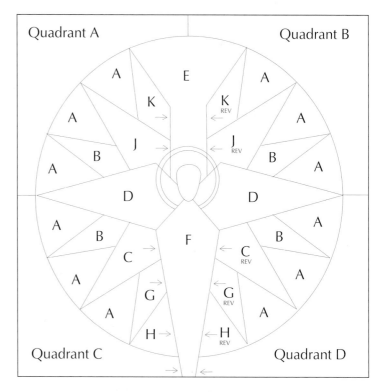

Fig 2

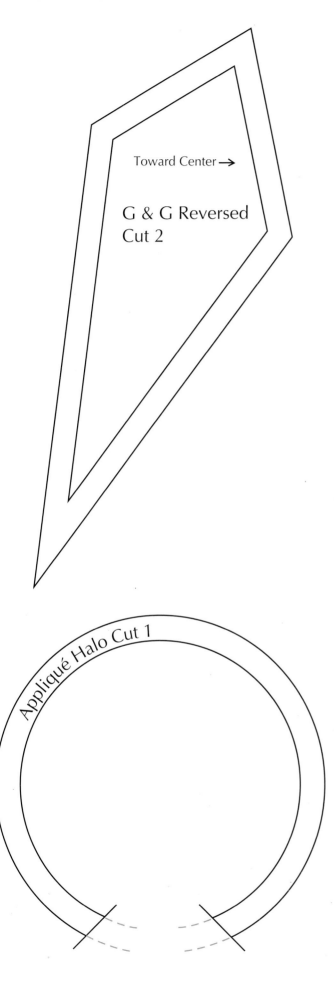

Toward Center →

G & G Reversed
Cut 2

Appliqué Halo Cut 1

Note: There are six templates with arrows (K, J, C, G, H, and lower frame). The arrow side of the template must face toward center.

1. Assemble each quadrant of the Mariner's Compass, noting that the upper left (Quadrant A) is the reverse of the upper right (Quadrant B). The lower left (Quadrant C) is the reverse of the lower right (Quadrant D).

2. Sew Quadrant A to the top background piece (Piece E), setting in the point where the top wing meets it.

3. Add the left wing (Piece D), setting in the corner.

4. Add Quadrant B, again setting in the upper point.

5. Sew right shoulder of Piece F to the right wing, (Piece D).

6. Join diagonal seam from left armpit to top of right wing. Then continue the seam, setting in the point.

7. Add Quadrant C, setting in the angle, and leaving the bottom of the angel's garment (Piece F) free about an inch above the circle

8. Add Quadrant D in the same manner.

9. Finish the block by setting the circle into the square frame. Complete the seams for the angel's garment.

Bottom Border:
These measurements include seam allowances.
Cut a striped piece of fabric, 20½" x 1". Stitch to bottom of angel block. Cut a piece of fabric, 20½" x 3", stitch to striped band.

Halo and Head:
These were appliquéd. Ends of the halos were tucked into a loosened seam. For extra dimension, cut a piece of batting the exact size of the head template and baste the fabric seam allowances over the batting piece before doing the appliqué.

Other Comments:
While we made a large display quilt for our six angels, you might consider a smaller size to accommodate a single angel and change the angel as the season or month changes. Velcro® attachments will make that easy to do. Put the "hook" part on the display quilt.

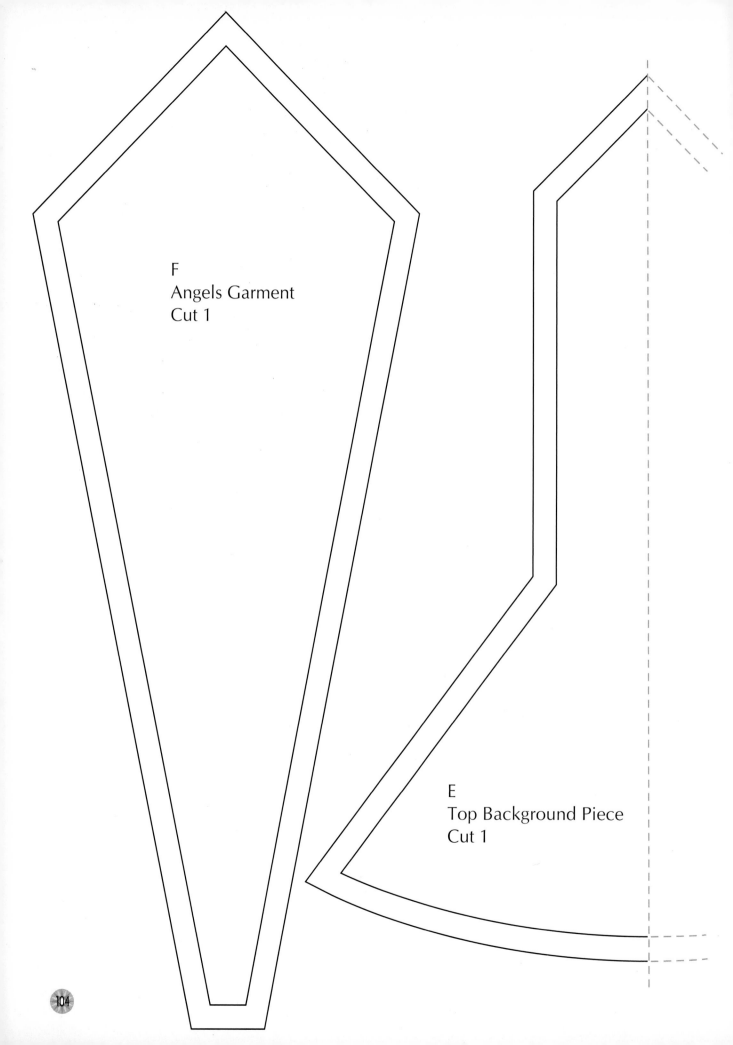

F
Angels Garment
Cut 1

E
Top Background Piece
Cut 1

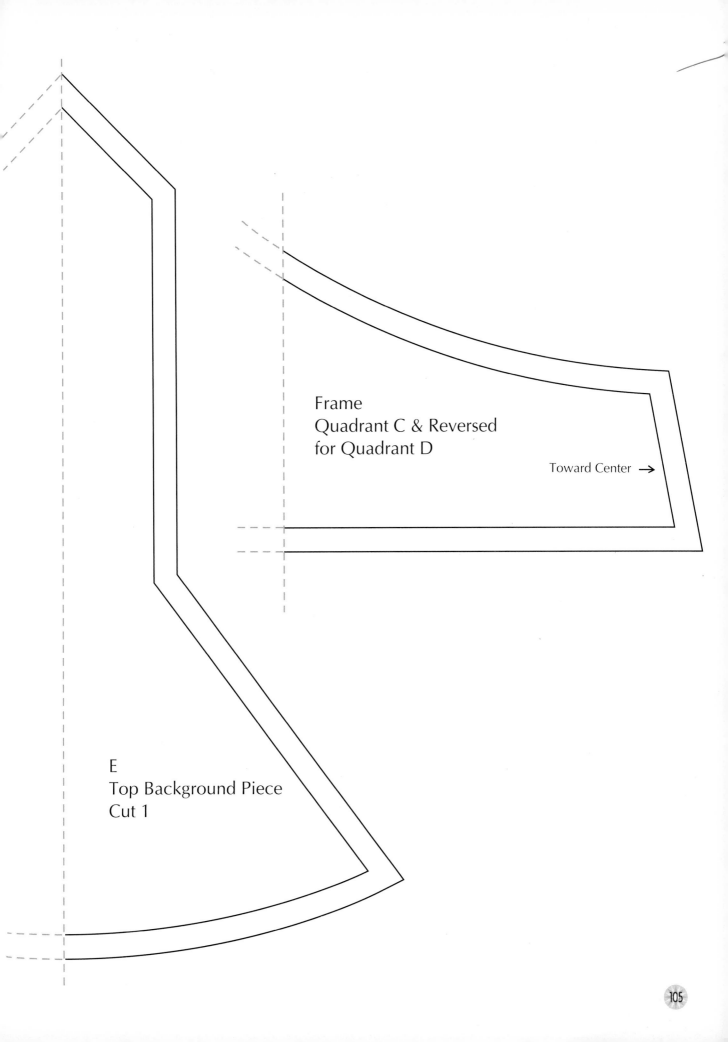

Frame
Quadrant C & Reversed
for Quadrant D

Toward Center →

E
Top Background Piece
Cut 1

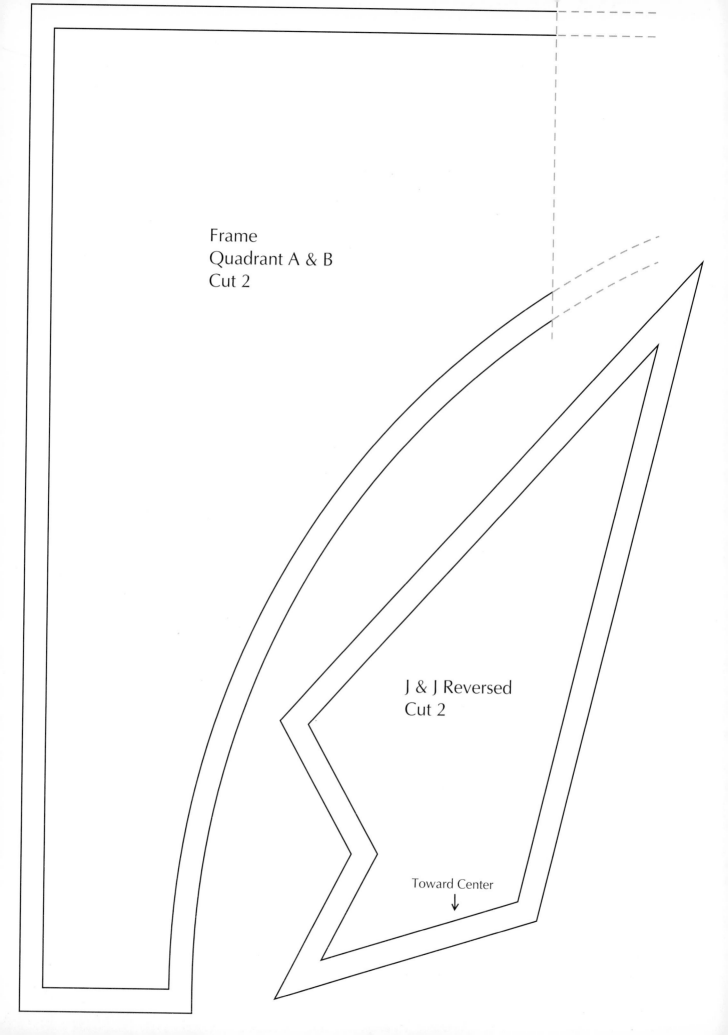

Frame
Quadrant A & B
Cut 2

J & J Reversed
Cut 2

Toward Center
↓

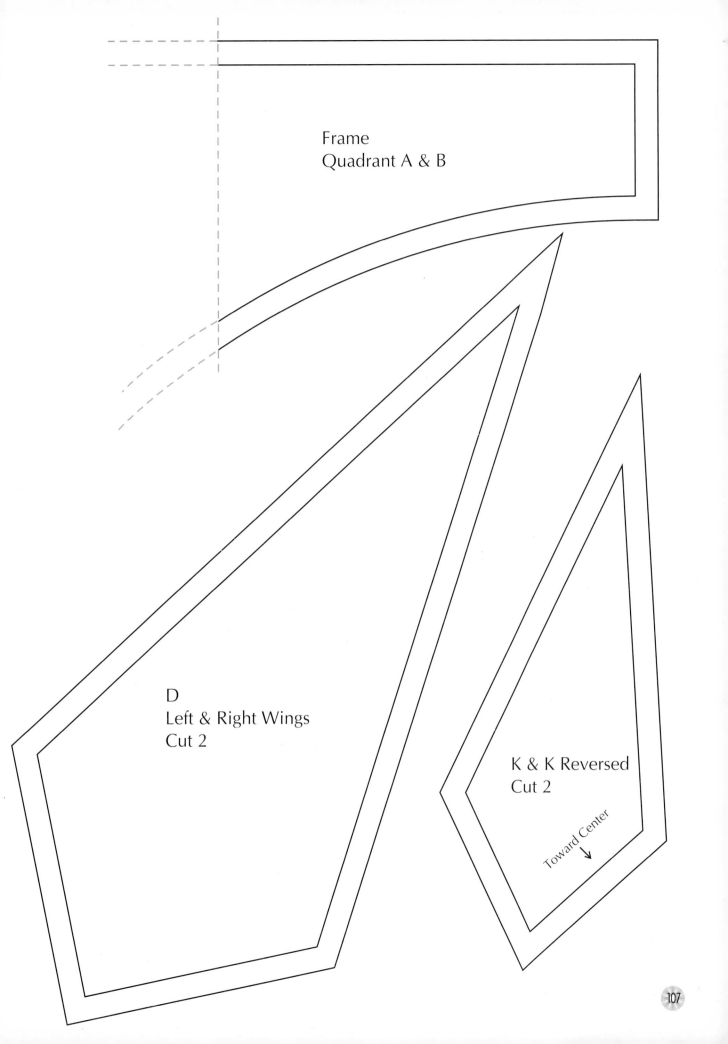

Frame
Quadrant A & B

D
Left & Right Wings
Cut 2

K & K Reversed
Cut 2

Toward Center

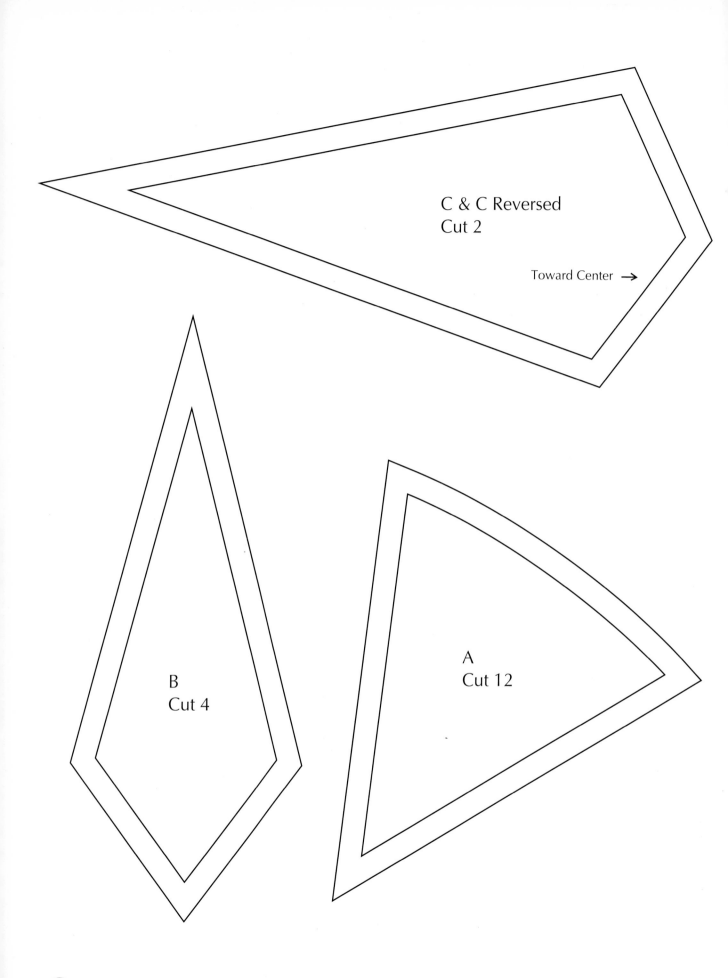

C & C Reversed
Cut 2

Toward Center →

B
Cut 4

A
Cut 12

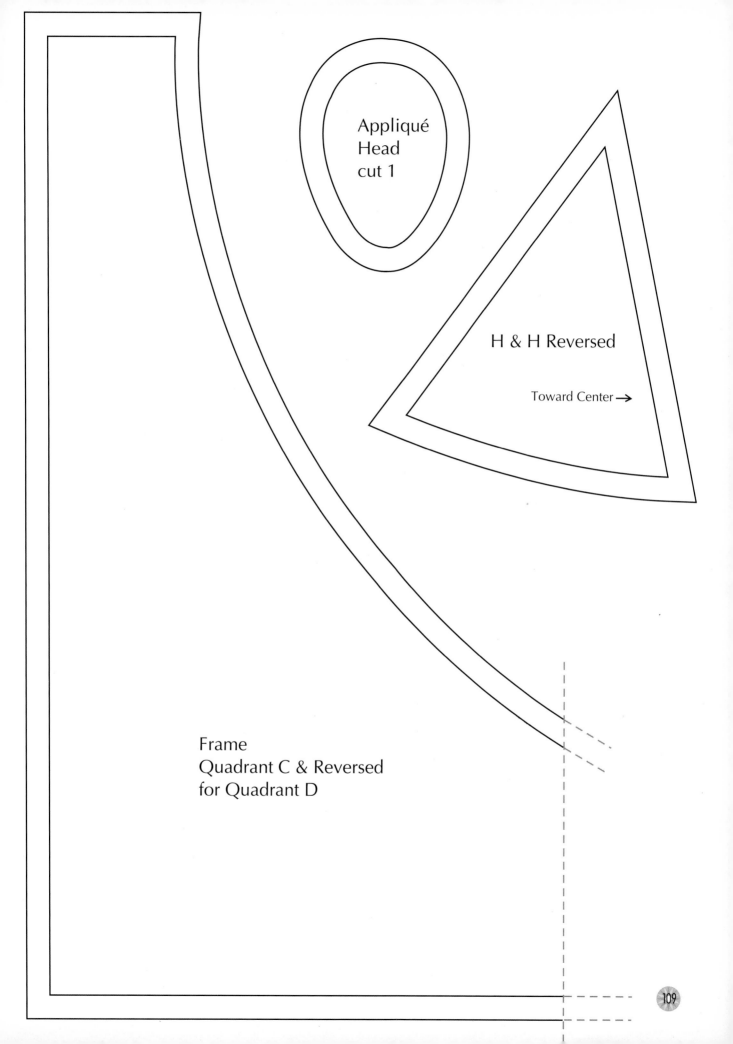

Appliqué
Head
cut 1

H & H Reversed

Toward Center →

Frame
Quadrant C & Reversed
for Quadrant D

The Quiltmakers

The Quilts

AQS BOOKS ON QUILTS

This is only a partial listing of the books on quilts that are available from the American Quilter's Society. AQS books are known the world over for their timely topics, clear writing, beautiful color photographs, and accurate illustrations and patterns. Most of the following books are available from your local bookseller, quilt shop, or public library. If you are unable to locate certain titles in your area, you may order by mail from the AMERICAN QUILTER'S SOCIETY, P.O. Box 3290, Paducah, KY 42002-3290. Customers with Visa or MasterCard may phone in orders from 7:00–5:00 CST, Monday–Friday, Toll Free 1-800-626-5420. Add $2.00 for postage for the first book ordered and $0.40 for each additional book. Include item number, title, and price when ordering. Allow 14 to 21 days for delivery.